Fit to Compete

 **Pelham Horsemaster Series**

Fit to Compete

Christine E. Hughes

Pelham Books

First published in Great Britain by
Pelham Books Ltd
44 Bedford Square
London WC1B 3DP
1985

British Library Cataloguing in Publication Data

    Hughes, Christine
        Fit to compete.— (Pelham horsemaster series)
    1. Horses
    I. Title
    636.1′083 SF285.3

ISBN 0-7207-1575-X

Typeset by Action Typesetting, Gloucester.
Printed in Great Britain by Hollen Street Press, Slough
and bound by Hunter & Foulis Ltd, Edinburgh

For my husband

Contents

Acknowledgments

I am indebted to several people who have made this book possible. First, my sincerest thanks for her guidance and encouragement from which my incentive and inspiration were born, go to Caroline Akrill without whose professional advice this book would never have been attempted. My husband deserves equal recognition for his untiring support to my selfish ambitions and to hours of proof-reading for what I hope he now feels has all been worthwhile. Bill Walter, my vet, checked the first two chapters for technical content, for which I am very grateful. Most importantly I want to thank the contributors to the second part of this book – the competitors themselves – who generously and patiently gave of their time and knowledge to enable me to document their methods. Hopefully in my attempt to illustrate their ideas of fittening and conditioning horses for equestrian sports I have not understated their skills. The wealth of knowledge so apparent in each of them deserves far more space than we have room for in this context and hopefully in the future they will find encouragement to express their own experiences.

This page would not be complete without mentioning Lesley Gowers whose shrewd foresight as an editor made my attempt as an author possible. She must be held responsible for persuading the publishers to take this work on board and for showing confidence in what I can only hope will prove worthwhile for everyone concerned.

Picture Acknowledgments

Unless otherwise credited all photographs have been taken by the author.

INTRODUCTION

In the chapters which follow I have attempted to demonstrate the principles of the horse's welfare which play a major part in preparing a horse for a series of competitions, and to interpret the various methods used by leading competitors for getting a horse fit for different equestrian disciplines. I make no apology for including details of their routines which some people may regard as trivial. No aspect of equine welfare should be considered as such, if, as a serious competitor, your priorities lie in achieving the peak of fitness with each horse you ride. Whilst we regard these sports for our own pleasure it must never be forgotten that a rider must be prepared to commit him- or herself utterly to the horse and all that competing involves. Whether we are weekend riders or professional competitors seeking financial reward the ultimate goal should be to enjoy optimum fitness and performance from your horse. There is nothing to be proud of in riding a fatigued or overstressed horse who has, through the rider's selfishness, been pushed beyond the level for which he has been prepared.

I have not endeavoured to categorise any horse for the sport in which he is participating because as many people will agree there can be no general fitness programmes for any horse or disciplines. Instead, I have taken case studies from seven of the most popular equestrian sports to illustrate principles from which we can develop our own fitness programmes to suit each horse. There is no deliberate attempt to favour any one sport and I hope I have not offended any equestrians by my choice. It is anticipated that readers will have an understanding of their horse's potential as a competitor and be capable of relating their own knowledge to a given situation whether caused by training or competition. It has not been considered necessary to explain how a horse is cared for but rather to highlight the importance of attending to all aspects. It is assumed that any aspiring competitor will already be a confident rider with enough common sense to apply training methods and a willingness to further his own knowledge.

Getting horses fit is all about increasing their physiological capacity to undergo more work without suffering undue fatigue and thereby achieving more efficient recovery rates. This can only be realised by gradually educating the body's system using a routine of planned exercise at certain paces with the aim of achieving a quality of fitness which, hopefully, will be demonstrated by improved performance. It must be clearly understood, and I hope sufficiently portrayed in the following chapters, that each discipline places different types of fitness demands on a horse. Therefore whilst preparing a horse for a chosen sport, he must not be expected to switch to another without appropriate alterations to his fitness programme and in good time. For example, a horse who is fit for show-jumping would not be safely able to negotiate a long-distance ride at short notice. I would hope that riders never abuse the horse for the sake of their own pleasure because it is not only the animal who suffers but also the sport. Common sense and a feeling for what you are trying to achieve are, after all, the practical interpretation of the theory you have learnt.

The response from many riders when asked how they get a horse fit is usually negative. Not that they don't wish to give away their own methods but rather that they actually 'play it by ear', and only afterwards stop and quantify a training programme in terms of miles of road work or minutes of schooling per day. Although I advocate flexibility throughout a training schedule in responding to each horse's reaction to a given routine, we should nevertheless draw up a detailed plan at the start with a specific goal in mind.

Whichever is the chosen equestrian sport the challenge of preparing a horse and competing will always inspire the keen rider to improve his performance each time he competes. The satisfaction of achieving peak fitness with every horse you ride should be as rewarding as any competition result. I hope that the following chapters will serve to inform the less knowledgeable and remind the experienced rider, who is perhaps contemplating trying his hand at a different discipline, of the importance of detail which this subject demands. By offering this book to you I hope that it will be judged by capable judges for it is not every equestrian who is a competent judge of some demonstrated truths.

PART ONE

1 Nutrition

This chapter is intended firstly to explain the principles of nutrition that should form the basic knowledge for anyone feeding horses who are expected to participate in competitions, and secondly to act as a foundation for the following chapters.

Nutrition is the process by which the various systems of the body are maintained in their normal form, composition, size and state of functioning. Therefore, in striving for optimum nutrition it is essential that each horse's energy and food requirements should be evaluated individually if we are to maintain a well-balanced ration in relation to the work programme. Unfortunately this is something that is often overlooked when trying to get horses fit on a restricted budget. This matter will be given further consideration in the next chapter.

To make up for the loss of substances in the performance of bodily functions and to obtain material for its other requirements the body receives nutrition in the form of food, water and oxygen. Food has to be digested before it becomes useful whilst water is absorbed unchanged and oxygen is drawn from the air by the lungs. Once the body has employed these materials to suit its needs any waste must be excreted efficiently through the skin, kidneys, lungs and intestines to enable the body's system to function in a healthy state. If these organs of excretion malfunction diarrhoea, constipation and indigestion can result.

The horse's digestive tract is quite different from that

of other animals insofar as the alimentary canal is relatively small and surrounded by muscular fibres which make it difficult for the horse to belch and impossible for him to vomit. Consequently whatever the horse eats must be kept moving through the system or the animal is liable to suffer from colic. As a comparison the size of a horse's stomach is something like 10–15 per cent of that of a cow, which is something that should be borne in mind when we quantify his daily ration.

The energy requirements of a horse are dictated by five factors:

1. Size
2. Temperament
3. Work
4. Environment
5. Age

The main supply of energy from food will come from the breakdown of starch in the small intestine and of fibre in the hind gut as well as from the excess of protein in the diet. The horse's condition is governed by the amount of starch and fibre in the food ration and will contribute to his energy requirements. Demands on his energy will increase as his fitness progresses so his daily ration must be adjusted accordingly, i.e. more concentrates and less hay.

Nutrients are drawn from the food to produce heat which the nervous system adapts to control the overall body temperature. Consequently as the atmosphere becomes colder more food will be utilised for maintaining body heat than for producing energy for work. This is where the use of clothing comes in but as there are other things to take into account on this subject it will be discussed in more detail in subsequent chapters. (See pages 51 and 52).

Food comprises various constituents which nourish

Composition of foods %

	Carbohydrates	Protein	Fat	Fibre	Minerals	Water	Digestibility
Oats	58.3	10.7	5.0	10.6	3.3	12.1	73
Barley	66.1	10.0	2.3	4.9	2.7	14.0	83
Bran	54.0	13.6	4.2	8.9	5.6	12.7	89
Maize	67.4	11.0	4.7	2.3	1.8	12.7	90
Beans	45.6	25.0	1.6	9.4	3.9	14.5	84
Sugar-beet	15.3	1.0	0.1	1.3	0.7	81.5	99
Linseed	10.6	20.5	37.0	7.2	3.4	12.3	86
Carrots	10.8	1.4	0.3	1.7	0.9	80.5	97
Apples	1.25	0.4	6.3	1.4	0.5	84.8	96
Meadow Hay	41.1	9.7	2.5	26.3	6.2	14.0	62
Seed Hay	36.1	10.2	2.7	30.2	6.3	14.3	55

the animal in different ways. These must be fed in proper proportions if the horse is to achieve peak fitness. It is therefore necessary to have an understanding of them and their effects on the body. The chief food constituents are: proteins, carbohydrates (sugar and starches), fats, salts, fibres, minerals, vitamins and water. The functions of each of these are as follows:

Proteins

All farm foods have protein in them although some such as root crops have very little. Peas, beans, oats, linseed and maize contain a relatively high proportion. Proteins are essential for an animal to live as well as work as they produce both heat and energy; they also repair muscular wastage and serve to build up tissues and organs. Excessive quantities of protein can cause colic, azoturia, diarrhoea, liver disorders, swollen legs (otherwise known as elephantitis), and can overheat the blood which causes the skin to erupt. On the other hand, a protein deficiency can result in depressed appetite, lack of stamina and loss of weight. The amount of protein in the diet in relation to fats, sugar and starches is known as the nitrogenous ratio and this varies in the adult horse from 1:5 in very hard worked animals to 1:10 in horses at rest.

Concentrated food groups can be categorised in the following way:

(a) Very high protein: fish meal; whole meat meal; blood meal.
(b) High protein: meat and bone meal; decorticated and undecorticated ground-nut cake; extracted soya-bean meal.
(c) Medium protein: linseed cake; beans; maize gluten meal; barley malt.
(d) Medium starchy: oats; wheat; rye; maize germ meal.
(e) Very starchy: barley; maize; flaked maize; dried sugar-beat pulp; rice meal; locust-bean meal; molasses.

The rough balancing of foods can be seen in the following table of nitrogenous ratios:

Food type	Ratios					
Very high protein					1	1
High protein			1	1		
Medium protein	1	2				
Starchy	1		3		6	
Very starchy		1		2		4

e.g. 1 part 'high protein' to 3 parts 'starchy' = balanced diet.

Carbohydrates
Carbohydrates are of prime importance for supplying energy which is required for growth maintenance and work therefore a lack of them would result in poor

condition and loss of weight. Starch is one of the main ingredients of most forms of food and together with sugar produces energy and helps maintain the body's temperature. Glucose, for example, is circulated all over the system, being broken down into carbon dioxide and water before generating a considerable amount of heat to the body. Foods which are high in starch content are oats, barley and maize, whereas carrots and apples have a very small amount. Although fats, sugar and starch cannot produce energy without the presence of protein, too large a proportion of carbohydrates reduces their digestibility.

Fats

Fats are present in all foods but in greatly varying quantities. They need much more oxidation (i.e. a larger amount of oxygen to break them down into carbon dioxide and water) than do carbohydrates before they can produce energy and heat. Any excess is built up to form body fat and if too much is given in the diet it can be harmful should the horse become overweight. The relation of fat to protein in the diet should be about one part fat to two and a half parts protein. This is known as the 'fatty ratio' which should always be given careful consideration when selecting a diet at any stage.

Salts

Salts, i.e. mainly potash, lime and soda, can be found in the blood, bones, muscle, hair, horn and sweat and in some fats. They play an important part in blood formation and food digestion although the body constantly excretes them through the skin, saliva, bowels and kidneys. They also play a part in helping the saliva and pancreatic juice to convert starch into sugar. A deficiency of salts produces tiredness which would manifest itself in a horse who has sweated a lot. It is therefore vital to ensure that horses are never deprived, especially when they are in work.

Crude Fibre

Crude fibre is that part of the food which is of a more or less woody nature. A certain amount of fibre is necessary in the diet of all horses except those under three and a half weeks of age when they are feeding on fluids only. Fibre supplies energy and helps towards the formation of fat while at the same time it provides essential bulk to the diet. It also acts as a mechanical aid in separating the concentrated foods, thus allowing the digestive juices to assist in absorbing nutrients into the system, and prevents foods from forming into a doughy mass. A balance must be found in supplying necessary fibre without displacing other nutrients.

It is worth mentioning here that a lack of fibre in the diet can be the cause of wood-chewing. It can also be blamed for causing pot-bellies when it is fed in excess because it passes undigested into the large intestine. For this reason care should be taken to ensure that horses in fast work do not become gross.

If we are to evaluate the true value of crude fibre in a ration an adjustment has to be made between the benefit derived from the digestible portion and the loss of energy incurred when dealing with the indigestible woody portion. Foods such as hay, straw and dried grass are all high in fibre content. Conversely, roots, maize and barley have very little fibre.

Minerals

The chief minerals essential in a horse's diet are: calcium, phosphorus, magnesium, potassium, chlorine, sodium and sulphur; plus the following: molybdenum, chromium, magnesium, selenium, iodine, copper, cobalt, iron and zinc. The latter group are known as 'trace elements' because they are needed only in relatively small amounts. Mineral matter is absolutely essential because it plays several roles which contribute to the well-being of the animal. In addition to building up bone in the growing animal it helps to maintain health and controls the rate of absorption of the digestive nutriments from the intestines. If the body does not receive sufficient minerals through the food it draws upon the bone and tissue for its supply. The same thing happens if too much of one and not enough of another is given. For most horses the optimum ratio of calcium: phosphorus that should be maintained is 1.1:1 to 2:1. These recommendations do not change with the amount of work the horse is doing. An imbalance of these two minerals, especially if phosphorus is in the excess, can cause the horse to suffer more than with any other mineral excess except salt. Phosphates are associated with calcium in the formation of bones and teeth so it follows that a deficiency of calcium causes softening of the bones and tooth decay.

The main factors governing the amount of minerals a horse actually needs are: his age – younger horses absorb minerals more efficiently; the general health and body weight; the growth rate – the faster the growth the more minerals are needed; and a tendency to sweat a lot. Bear in mind also that some horses appear to absorb minerals more easily than others. The amount of minerals present in the soil will also influence the horse's intake. Common foodstuffs such as oats, barley, maize and bran are all lacking in calcium but contain a relatively high proportion of phosphorus. It may therefore be necessary to supplement the diet with either ground limestone, steamed bone flour, calcium lactate, calcium gluconate or dicalcium phosphate.

Vitamins

These substances are found in natural foods so it is generally considered that if a horse is feeding under natural conditions he will, in normal circumstances, find all the vitamins he needs. Vitamins not only assist in the utilisation of various nutrients in promoting normal health and growth but are also vital for the horse's metabolism. A horse will need more vitamins and minerals as his workload increases. The most important vitamins together with their main sources and symptoms of deficiency are:

	Source	*Deficiency Symptoms*
Vitamin A	Green food Carrots Green pasture Quality hay Cod liver oil	Unthriftiness Hoof lesions Night blindness Respiratory ailments Corneal lesions
Vitamin B1, 2, 12	Cereals Yeast Beans Egg yolk Some fruit and vegetables	General debility
Vitamin C	Glucose Most fruit and vegetables	Unthriftiness
Vitamin D	Sunshine Milk Green crops Animal and vegetable oil Egg yolk	Bony enlargements Rickets
Vitamin E	Wheat germ	Infertility

The following table gives a rough guide to the comparative vitamin content of common feedstuffs.

	A	B	C	D	E
Oats	1	2	0	0	3
Barley	1	2	0	0	3
Bran	1	3	0	0	2
Maize	0	2	0	0	2
Beans	1	2	1	0	0
Sugar beet	0	0	0	0	0
Linseed	1	2	0	0	2
Carrots	3	2	3	0	0
Apples	1	2	3	0	0
Meadow hay	2	2	1	2	2
Seed hay	2	2	1	3	3

0 = none; 1 = small amount; 2 = moderate amount; 3 = rich.

Water

Nutrition of the body is performed by fluids, i.e. blood, saliva, bile and gastric juices which cannot act efficiently unless an adequate proportion of water is maintained. In the body, water stimulates changes of tissue and assists in the removal of carbonic acid. This gas in the water increases the solubility of carbonate of lime and consequently aids nutrition. Water is present in all food-stuffs but the percentage can vary from as little as 10 − 12 per cent in oats to 80-90 per cent in carrots. From this we can see how much the type of food in the diet affects the horse's water consumption.

Drinking water is, in fact, the most vital nutrient of all because horses cannot survive as long without water as they can without food. They will soon start to lose weight if they are deprived of a constant supply and if it is restricted at all less food will be eaten and vice versa. The more minerals a horse consumes, especially salt, the thirstier he will become. Without enough fluid in the body, animals are unable to replenish the loss which occurs through secretion of saliva and digestive juices or by excretion through the skin (sweat) and kidneys (urine). A shortage therefore restricts the production of both flesh and work.

From the foregoing breakdown of nutrients we can see how important it is to analyse each horse's type, size, age, temperament, living conditions and work programme before arriving at the most suitably balanced ration. Obviously some horses will be easier to get fit than others: for instance, a cob who has been at grass for several months will take longer to walk off the excess of fat that has built up before he can begin faster work, than will a more naturally athletic Thoroughbred type in the same circumstances. We should therefore reduce the cob's intake of fatty foods at the outset of his fitness programme. The Thoroughbred, on the other hand, will have a lighter skeletal frame and is less likely to carry too much weight once he has started work. His temperament will usually be more sensitive too, and will often react more markedly to a change of lifestyle and/or diet.

Nutritional deficiencies can cause emaciation, poor bone development and slow healing, apart from reducing energy and stamina. Specific forms of malnutrition depend on the lack of certain elements in the diet, such as proteins, vitamins or minerals. It may even be a combination of any of these, making the diagnosis even more difficult. For this reason it is always advisable to call your veterinary surgeon who will examine the animal and prescribe treatment.

Nutritional ailments may be caused by the deficiencies just mentioned or by improper feeding or watering, or can follow an infection. Also an incorrect ratio of diet to work can be seriously harmful. Such disorders will show themselves mostly in the forms that have previously been suggested such as colic or azoturia and may be overcome by supplementing the feed. Any persistence in the symptoms must, however, be taken seriously and your vet advised.

Our prime consideration must be to achieve peak fitness in whichever sport we are participating in and clearly we cannot do this without keeping the horse in perfect condition. Nutrition is a feature of the horse's welfare over which we have almost complete control. Once we have an understanding of his dietary requirements it is up to us to ensure we have done everything in our power to supply him with the nutrients he will need throughout the various stages of his training.

2 Feeding

The principles of feeding should become second nature to us all so that whatever situation the horse endures during his competitive life, his feeding programme can be varied without causing him undue distress. The first thing to remember is that water should always be made available before feeding because a horse drinks large gulps fairly quickly and the water goes into the water-gut via the stomach and small bowel. Therefore a quantity of water taken immediately after a meal would wash into the bowel some of the stomach contents, which would not be adequately mixed with gastric juices. As a result of the food not being sufficiently digested at this stage, indigestion or colic are likely to occur. Likewise, hard work directly after a feed should be strictly avoided because a full stomach will press against the diaphragm and lungs restricting their power to expand. This naturally causes the horse to become distressed and blow. The lungs are then in danger of becoming choked with blood and the digestion might be halted, resulting in chronic colic which could prove fatal.

A horse's digestive system is so arranged that he may feed continuously for many hours, as he would in natural conditions, rather than take in a large quantity at any one time. The small size of his stomach dictates that he should be fed in small quantities, frequently. Ideally he should have his ration divided into three meals and any increase in quantity should be give as an additional meal rather than adding it to an existing one.

Horses soon become used to a routine, which should

be respected by those who care for them. If this responsibility is not taken seriously, there is always a danger of the horse becoming irritable if he is made to wait for his feed. After all, whilst he is stabled he is totally at your mercy and cannot be blamed if any annoyance on his part leads to stable vices which in turn can impair his fitness. Horses will respond differently to the time they are fed but the benefit gained from leaving them to eat their meal in peace and quiet cannot be emphasised enough. In fact some horses will not eat their feed at all if there is activity in the stable yard after feed-time. It is quite common for a horse to wait until late into the evening to finish his meal but this should not be used as an excuse to unnecessarily attend to him straight after rather than before he is fed.

Experience of feeding, which develops into an art, comes only through practice and an understanding of the horse's condition whatever his stage of fitness. To be able to relate this to his work and dietary requirements is a real skill, for no two horses will respond in the same way. Anyone can mix a bucket of food and empty it into a manger but it takes a conscientious person to recognise the need for an adjustment in the ration. Under-feeding or over-feeding are always a danger if one does not have an understanding of the effects of the various feedstuffs and the ways that they can be fed. It is often heard that 'kindness' can result in actual harm if large portions of high-energy foods are fed to a horse that is out of work. Food in excess of the horse's needs can cause diarrhoea and fermentation in the bowels, resulting in poisons being absorbed into the sytsem. Colic and azoturia are other common results of over-feeding with high-energy food. The former can lead to a twisted gut, which is fatal.

On the other hand, under-feeding of any food is also harmful. In particular, feeding insufficient energy foods to meet the horse's needs will result in a lack of performance from a drop, however minimal, in condition. Even in resting horses who only require a maintenance diet, under-feeding of energy foods during cold weather can prove fatal if the body temperature drops too far below normal.

The digestibility of food is determined by its quality, quantity, combination and water content, together with the health and age of the horse and the work he is doing. This is reduced by any lack of fibre and bulky food, which leads to general debility and loss of condition.

Palatability is controlled by the amount of food, its texture and taste. No matter how selective we are when buying feedstuffs, there will invariably be some dust content in the food, particularly in oats, barley and bran, and this will effect palatability. This can be counteracted by damping slightly with water when mixing the feed. Care must be taken not to wet the feed too much as this will cause it to form into a doughy, unappetising mass.

Palatability is also reduced if a food has been allowed to become mouldy or polluted by vermin. Either would create an offensive smell and soon put a horse off his feed.

Another contributory factor with regard to the palatability of food is the cleanliness of the horse's manger, feed buckets or indeed any utensil which is used for food. Mangers should be cleaned at least twice a week with hot water. Any left-overs must be removed promptly because they will soon adopt an offensive odour and contaminate the manger. Don't be surprised if your horse goes off his food if you haven't washed his manger for several days. Wooden mangers are the most difficult to keep clean because the food becomes ingrained in the wood. You will need a bucketful of hot water and a very stiff scrubbing brush to loosen the stale food before wiping clean with a sponge or cloth. If the manger is removable it is much simpler to leave it to soak before rinsing clean. As with all cleaning jobs they are much easier if you do them regularly. Feed buckets should be washed out immediately after feeding which again is no job at all if it's done thoroughly every time.

If buckets are to be used as a manger, they must be removed once the horse has finished eating to avoid any possibility of accident.

Food bins which are used for storage are best swept out before refilling them with fresh food. This ensures that no stale or damp food is allowed to gather in the bottom of the bin, and contamination of the new supplies is avoided. Dampness will almost invariably seep up through the bottoms of bins which are standing directly on the ground. To prevent this, stand them on blocks of wood or place a brick under each corner. If food is stored in sacks, again be sure they are kept off the ground. This is particularly important with paper sacks as these will rot quickly and pounds of food could be wasted. Sugar-beet pulp is especially susceptible to damp conditions and will soon form moulds making it unsafe to feed.

There are a number of points to take into account when considering any change in a horse's diet. Firstly, that the breakdown of fibre in the large intestine is carried out by bacteria and any dietary changes should be made gradually to enable the bacteria to adjust according to the type of food, otherwise the digestive process cannot be performed efficiently. Secondly, the feeding value of the food must be evaluated (see page 19). Thirdly, the balance of food and its nitrogenous ratio (page 20). And finally, the price of feedstuffs, which cannot be ignored.

Some horses will take longer to adapt to a new diet than others, especially delicate feeders, in which case it may be a good idea to disguise the new food by mixing in chopped apples and carrots. Likewise, supplements and additives such as cod liver oil may have to be introduced gradually to avoid putting a horse off his feed. As a last resort cod liver oil can be squirted onto the back of the tongue with a syringe. Often, horses who are otherwise good feeders will turn up their nose at a mash. This can usually be overcome by offering it in small portions laced with carrots, apples or a handful of grass. If you still can't persuade the horse to eat, you may have to feed him by hand. It is a mistake to have a mash too wet, in fact all feeds should be of a crumbly texture to make them most palatable.

If an otherwise healthy horse is not eating normally and you have already considered the points above, check his teeth carefully. So often, sharp or uneven wear of the molars can be the cause of a horse not thriving because he has been unable to chew his food properly. Rough edges on the teeth can cause mouth sores on the tongue and gums which will make it painful for the horse to eat and if not dealt with promptly can cause him to lose condition. Such a setback in the fitness programme can be easily avoided if the teeth are checked regularly and rasped at least once a year as a matter of routine. This is particularly relevant in older horses whose teeth wear more unevenly than do those of youngsters and are more prone to abscesses.

Having an understanding of nutrition is the basis on which we can formulate a diet. We must now look into the other factors which contribute to dietary requirements. These can be subdivided into body maintenance needs and working needs. Bearing in mind the total appetite of an animal we must firstly ensure that the working needs are supplied with concentrated foods before satisfying the appetite with the maintenance needs, which will most likely be in the form of hay or grass. These will, of course, vary from horse to horse depending on the work which is required of him, his appetite and how efficiently his digestive system converts the foodstuffs.

Maintenance levels are chiefly governed by the skin surface of the animal, i.e. the larger the skin surface area, the more heat will be lost through radiation which will have to be replaced by food. Any increase of atmospheric temperature lessens the need for heat maintenance in the body resulting in fat production. The temperament of the horse will also play a part; more highly strung animals will burn up food in nervous energy.

Whether the horse is clipped or not, his clothing and how he is housed will be added factors to consider. But the work programme is the main influence on his dietary requirements. This can be broken down into three categories:

(a) type
(b) intensity
(c) duration

These three aspects will be discussed in the following chapters.

The time of year will play a significant part in the horse's daily allowance of food if he is to be turned out at all during his training schedule. Springtime will bring new grass growing rapidly and some pastures are richer than others depending on their management. There is naturally less goodness in the grass during the winter months so it would have to be substituted completely with hay, in most cases from autumn through to the spring. A horse will soon put on weight if he is allowed to have too much grass on top of his concentrated diet. This will affect his wind and consequently his state of fitness and must therefore be watched closely. As in humans, obesity can cause heart conditions and filled legs.

We shall now consider the most common types of foodstuffs available and the different ways in which they can be fed.

Oats

Oats are traditionally the most popular food for horses. As in all farm-produced grain they do vary in quality so be sure to choose those which are free from impurities. They should be clean, bright, plump, free from dust, and should rattle when shaken. They can be fed bruised, rolled or crushed depending on preference, but bear in mind that the more they are flattened, the dustier they will become. Once they have been crushed, they must be used within four weeks in winter and two weeks in summer. They can be fed whole but this tends to encourage the horse to bolt them rather than chew them slowly, and therefore chaff (chopped hay) should be mixed with them to aid digestion. Alternatively, they can be boiled in the same way as barley. Oats are best not used in their year of harvest.

Barley

Look for much the same qualities as in oats. They are often fed crushed or boiled whole after being soaked overnight in cold water. The grain swells up during cooking so keep it covered with plenty of water to prevent it boiling dry and forming a solid mass. A clothes boiler is ideal for cooking grain but if left to boil dry, the heating elements will soon become damaged. After three to four hours the grain will split open and become soft, making it ready to feed together with its valuable juices. Care should be taken with all boiled feed that it is not fed too hot otherwise the horse could burn his tongue and be put off his feed. It should be fed at blood heat after being mixed into a crumbly texture with the rest of the feed.

Dried Sugar-beet Pulp

Unlike oats and barley this is a root crop which is processed in a factory before being sold loose or in cube form. Either way it has been dried, and if fed without being soaked for a minimum of twenty-four hours in at least double its own volume of water, it will swell up in the horse's stomach and quickly cause colic. Care should be taken when making up large quantities of sugar-beet, to use a container which is large enough to allow for thorough soaking, mixing and expansion. Fatalities in horses have been recorded as a result of careless soaking of sugar-beet, so do beware if you leave the job to others. Sugar-beet is, however, a highly digestible food and useful for putting on weight.

Bran

The broadest bran, although difficult to find today, is preferred because it is less dusty and consequently more palatable. Be sure to dampen just before feeding, just enough to form a crumbly texture as too much water will make it distasteful. It aids digestion and because of its laxative properties it is the main ingredient of bran mashes which are given to horses the evening before their rest day or to those sick and out of work.

Flaked Maize

Again this should be free from dust, damp or any odour, be as fresh as possible and have a bright yellow colour. It is a high energy food and should be fed in moderation, particularly at the start of a training programme, to avoid overheating of the blood.

Linseed

Look for grains which are clean, shiny, pure and plump. It can be stored for many months if housed in a cool, dry place; otherwise it will become poisonous if subjected to a warm or damp atmosphere. Apart from its value as a laxative, which can be utilised in mashes, it also improves the condition and bloom of the horse's coat. For this reason it is beneficial to horses in work and can be fed daily in small portions, i.e. no more than 10 per cent of the total daily ration.

To prepare linseed for a meal, take one handful per horse and soak it overnight in cold water before bringing it to the boil the next morning. Then leave it to simmer until the evening feed-time. Take care when bringing it to the boil as it will quickly boil over and apart from the loss this will incur, it is very difficult to clean up. After serving the linseed, any left-overs should be discarded and a fresh brew prepared thereafter; it will not keep once cooked. Likewise if the horse does not eat it up within a couple of hours, be sure to clean out his manger thoroughly to avoid contaminating his next feed. Very often barley is cooked with the linseed which lessens the likelihood of boiling over. A ratio of three to seven parts barley to one part linseed is a general guide only and subject to the same variations as other rations.

Beans

The type of beans suitable for horses are hard, plump, dry and sweet, and they must be cracked before feeding. Look out for weevils and mites attacking them during storage. They contain more nutritive materials than oats and for this reason can cause overheating of the blood if fed in excess. Young beans are less nutritious and therefore more likely to cause colic and flatulence than those over twelve months old. Because of their protein content they are only usually fed to horses in very hard work.

Carrots

Carrots have a relatively high vitamin A, B and C content. Often, bought carrots will be pre-washed; if not, be sure to do this to satisfy yourself that they are free from slugs and insects. Feed them whole, or sliced lengthways to avoid the risk of choking. Store them in a dry place as any damp will soon form mould and rot them.

Apples

Cut into quarters before feeding. Never feed any which are starting to rot. As with carrots they are very useful for tempting a delicate feeder or simply to make a feed more appetising.

Salt

All horses should have a regular supply of salt to help purify the blood and assist in ridding the animal of intestinal worms. It also increases the thirst, so if rock salt is fed *ad lib,* water must be constantly available. A tablespoon of common salt in the feed once a day will normally be enough for the average horse.

Epsom Salts

These are particularly beneficial for use as a laxative. A handful mixed into a feed or mash once each week acts as a safeguard against constipation.

Bicarbonate of Soda

This can be used for the same reasons as in man. If flatulence is suspected, a dessertspoonful given either in the feed or in water will generally ease the condition. Any persistence of the symptoms should be reported to your vet because they could be a sign of illness.

Molasses

Most feed merchants sell either molassine meal or liquid molasses, the latter being usually more economical. Molasses are the crude and less expensive form of black treacle and are fed for their sugar content, and as an appetiser. One handful of meal or three to four tablespoons of liquid per day also increases the palatability of a meal.

Mashes

A mash is the easiest and most common form of feeding a laxative, which the stabled horse will need once if not twice a week. It ensures that his system is free from any congestion and subsequently acts as a prevention against any digestive disorders. Not only is it useful for giving the working horse a change from his diet of concentrates, giving his digestive organs a brief rest, but it is essential for sick or resting animals. There are three forms of mashes most commonly used in the stable. They are:

     (a) bran only
     (b) bran and oats
     (c) bran and linseed

To make a basic bran mash (a), fill a bucket with one third to two thirds of bran, depending on the horse's requirements, pour on boiling water, add one handful of Epsom salts, three to four tablespoons of liquid molasses (or a handful of molassine meal) and mix very thoroughly.

For type (b) follow the same method as above, adding oats before mixing.

A linseed mash (c) is made up of the same ingredients as the plain bran mash but with boiled linseed added before mixing.

All mashes, once mixed, must be covered and left to cool until at blood heat before feeding. As with other feeds, a crumbly texture is the ideal consistency.

Cubes

There is such a wide choice of cubes available these days for every horse and its work programme that to write about each one could easily fill a chapter. But generally speaking, if you feed cubes only as the concentrate part of the diet, some succulent food will be necessary to aid digestion and add variety. Each type of cube is analysed for you to study before choosing the one to match the horse's demands. Whichever type you select, be sure to follow the manufacturer's recommendations with regard to quantity. Although cubes are a convenience food, we should not allow that factor to influence our choice of diet.

Hay

Hay is a relatively broad-based description of conserved grass, dried either by natural or artificial methods or a combination of both. It therefore follows that its nutritional value is as variable as the grass from which it is made. Hay is usually described as meadow hay or seed hay. Meadow hay, being made from permanent pasture, is probably softer, sweeter, shorter and contains a wide variety of herbage, but may be short on fibre. Seed hay is made from one-, two-, or three-year-old grasses in which rye grass predominates. These tend to be longer and leafier, consequently more fibrous and probably higher in protein. Essential qualities of hay are palatability, a pleasing aroma, good fibre content without being 'woody' and complete freedom from dust and mould. It will provide a basic food balance for body maintenance. The type and quality a horse needs will be calculated the same way as with concentrated foods, i.e. type, intensity and duration of work. The more fast work he does as his fitness programme progresses the less hay he should have. Good quality hay is crucial for horses in work because lesser quality will affect the horse's respiration.

There are several methods of feeding hay but whichever way you choose, make sure that the portion is shaken up thoroughly to check it carefully for thistles, mouldy patches, foreign bodies and even dead mice (who didn't see the baler coming). If the hay is at all dusty, sprinkle it with water, preferably using a watering-can fitted with a sprinkler. Some horses need their hay completely soaked in water before feeding as dry hay irritates them. If you use hay-nets do keep them in good repair; any large holes should be darned with string. Always use a quick-release knot and tie the net high enough so the horse cannot catch a leg in it, particularly when the net is empty. Hay racks and deep mangers are probably the safest and least wasteful means of feeding hay. Hay fed on the floor will often be used partly for bedding by wasteful horses. However, if you have a horse with nasal congestion, feeding hay on the floor allows his nasal passages to drain freely.

If you are unable to make hay off your own paddocks, buying from your nearest farmer is usually less expensive than from a merchant.

Hay should be stored in a dry, well-ventilated barn to prevent it from over-heating.

Haylage or Vacuum-packed Hay

Haylage is a specially prepared feed, so called because it is half-way between hay and silage. It is a relatively new alternative to conventional hay and among its more common trade names are Horsehage and Propack. In its simplest form haylage is made by cutting young grass or lucerne and, before it has completely wilted, packing it into sealed plastic bags. These bags are quite heavy because of the moisture content of the grass and consequently the handling is more difficult. At the moment it is a comparatively expensive commodity and its quality is variable because it relies both on the time at which the grass was cut and on the efficiency of packing it into plastic bags which must be airtight. Its shelf life is somewhat shorter than that of traditional hay and whilst it can be stored outdoors there is always a danger that the bags could be punctured, which would effectively render the contents useless. Vermin are another threat and once they contaminate haylage, wastage is inevitable. Haylage is, however, highly digestible and its protein content is greater than that of normal hay. It is probably only economical for horses with sensitive digestions or respiratory ailments.

Supplements
The question of supplementary feeding cannot be taken too seriously and if you are in any doubt it will not only save the horse from an imbalance in his diet, but also your pocket if you seek professional advice before stocking your feed shed with unnecessary and invariably expensive additives and supplements. Unfortunately there are those who, under advice, have bought a quantity of a particular supplement for one horse and will then feed it to other horses believing it can't do them any harm, rather than pausing to consider their individual dietary requirements. So always satisfy yourself that a horse actually needs a different form of food before you waste your money. There are today a wide range of products available which cater for every vitamin and mineral deficiency in the horse. However, we should beware. These products tend to go through phases of popularity depending on the success of the manufacturer's marketing. Never allow yourself to be talked into

buying a product just because it seems fashionable. Do consult your vet, who will be able to advise you on the best product to suit your horse's needs.

Watering

As mentioned in the first chapter, the horse's diet will constantly influence his thirst, as will the climate, but generally speaking a healthy stabled horse will drink five to ten gallons a day. It is therefore essential that he should be allowed a constant supply so that he will not drink too much at any one time. It may be found that one bucketful is not enough to last him through the night, in which case give him an extra one last thing at night. The only times that a horse should not have water *ad lib* are immediately before and after fast work. When a horse is tired, he should be offered a small amount of tepid water rather than cold water because after work he may not have enough vitality to warm a quantity of cold water to the temperature of his body and therefore he would be more susceptible to catching a chill. This in turn could upset his bowels, resulting in more serious illnesses. After a competition, and once he has completely cooled down, he may be allowed a short drink before a journey. But a large quantity at this stage could cause colic as he will be standing still for some time. The subject of watering during some types of competitions will be dealt with in later chapters.

Automatic watering bowls in the stable are becoming increasingly popular in place of buckets because they are a labour-saving device. However, the author is not in favour of their use for the following reasons. Firstly, and most importantly, we are unable to measure a horse's water intake and subsequently monitor any changes – often this can be a first indication of ill-health. Secondly, if a horse needs to receive any medicines via his water, he is more likely to accept them diluted in a bucket containing two gallons than in an automatic bowl which only holds about three or four pints. If you have a horse who kicks over his bucket, fix a metal holder to the wall at about manger height and set the bucket in it. Fasten the handle of the bucket down so that the bucket cannot be removed. Do not be tempted to top up the bucket instead of changing it for fresh water – which should be done at least three times a day. Standing water will absorb impurities from the air and if neglected can be a source of disease. Whatever receptacle you use, it must be cleaned daily to avoid slime forming.

Feed Chart
Whether you are feeding one or many horses, and whether they are stabled or not, it is imperative that an up-to-date feed chart is kept. A blackboard serves the purpose ideally but a piece of wood painted matt black will do the job just as well. Alternatively cardboard or paper, pinned up in the feed shed, detailing every part of each horse's diet, including the hay quota, will ensure that whoever is responsible for the feeding need not make mistakes. Any alterations in a horse's diet should be noted on the feed chart no matter how temporary they may be. Failure to do this could result in a resting horse being fed his normal concentrated ration instead of a laxative diet. The consequences of such a mistake manifest themselves most commonly through colic or azoturia.

One thing is certain as far as feeding horses is concerned: ignorance is *not* bliss and if you have any doubts whatsoever, seek expert advice because if you have never fed a horse before you will need guidance. Remember, when feeding horses attention to detail is the sign of a good horseman, and no consideration is too small.

3 Stable Management

Whichever equestrian sport you choose any success will be the result of months of hard work both on and off the horse. All aspects of equine welfare rely on a dedicated and conscientious attitude and no more so than in the management of the stable yard and its residents. There are many elements which belong under this heading and it cannot be over emphasised that every subject in this chapter deserves equal attention. Sadly, though, standards of stable management vary from one yard to the next, unfortunately to the detriment of the horse. This is so often due to lack of self-discipline or ignorance on the part of the owner but there are no excuses for the uninitiated not to seek professional advice. No matter how broad our knowledge there is always room for extending it. This chapter will therefore venture to remind those responsible of the importance of a high standard whenever horses are involved.

To establish a routine which primarily evolves around the horse's welfare is the basis on which all other aspects of stable life revolve. The importance of a feeding routine has already been pointed out in the last chapter, and the same rule applies to the rest of the stable duties because horses thrive on a uniformed life-style. So often stable vices develop if this is not respected. Regard should also be given to the atmosphere which the staff create in the yard because animals are particularly sensitive to human temperament. Indeed a horse's character can be seriously affected in response to his handler's mis-management through ill-temper. As well as ensuring that the horses are relaxed and content, a stable yard cannot operate efficiently without a routine. An organised yard reflects the dedication and team effort of those who care about the welfare and ultimate success of their charges.

The fundamental aspects which comprise a stable routine are the same for horses in any competitive discipline. The early morning chores of mucking-out and setting-fair the boxes, feeding, changing rugs and bandages, and brushing over the horses are normally carried out before breakfast, as is the general tidying of the yard. Some riders may choose to ride before breakfast, particularly during the hot summer months when flies are a problem. In this case the horse is fed after he has worked if there isn't enough time for him to digest a meal before exercise. After breakfast the morning is usually taken up with working the horses. How much time you have to attend to them afterwards will depend on whether or not you have staff and how many horses you have to work. Some people prefer to groom horses whilst they are still warm because their pores are open and as a consequence they are easier to clean more thoroughly. On the other hand if you have a busy schedule a quick brush over or a sponge down will ensure the horse is comfortable until you have time to groom him properly later in the day. A sweaty horse should never be left to dry on his own though; once he has been washed down it is up to you to ensure that he has dried off and is rugged up comfortably before being left. Some horses are prone to breaking out into a cold sweat after work which can lead to a chill if care is not taken in drying them off. The weather will, of course, make all the difference as to how you deal with a warm and sweaty horse. If you have nowhere to lead him out to dry off, then rubbing either with a stable rubber or straw will do the job. Always make sure that his ears and legs are dried thoroughly and, if necessary, bandage his legs with woollen wraps. Leave him with enough clothing on to ensure that his normal body temperature will be maintained. Take care to avoid any draughts and, if helpful, close the top door of the stable for a while. If you have any doubts about his recovery from exercise do not leave him for more than ten minutes at a time because this is when he is most likely to show symptoms of distress which must be relieved immediately. 'Tying up' and colic, apart from a common cold which can lead to pneumonia, are but some of the immediate dangers threatening a fatigued horse who has been neglected. Sufficient time to recover should be allowed after the horse has worked so that he does not arrive in the stable yard still blowing. His legs should be checked for any wounds, heat or swelling and feet should be picked out before he is left. The slightest suspicion of 'a leg' should be treated immediately no matter how time-consuming. So often a 'stitch in time saves nine'.

If you do make it a practice to turn the horses out after work they will probably be given a ration of hay when they come in. Some people choose to feed a portion of hay before the horse is worked and others prefer to have hay constantly available. This is a matter of personal preference depending on the horse's work. It does, however, make no sense at all to expect a horse to do any fast work on a full stomach of hay – his respiration could be seriously endangered.

Before feeding at lunch-time, horses should be checked over, the beds skepped out and water in the buckets renewed. If all the horses have finished work for the day, the afternoon is usually taken up with grooming, tack-cleaning, clipping and trimming, as well as yard maintenance and the many miscellaneous duties which ensure the smooth running of a competition yard.

The evening stables, or 'doing-up' time as it is known,

basically involves changing water, rugs, perhaps bandages, any veterinary treatment, skepping-out the beds, giving hay, and, finally, when the yard is tidy, feeding. The last chore should be feeding so that the horses can be left to eat in peace.

Even if there are no horses to be given a night feed, it is always advisable to check them, say, between 9 and 10 p.m. Rugs may need adjusting, even if the horse is otherwise comfortable and has eaten up his last feed. Droppings should be picked up and water topped up before the horse is left for the night.

Throughout the day, as a matter of habit, you should feel the horse's legs so that any abnormality is spotted and any necessary action taken. There should always be a skep to hand so that each time you enter a stable, droppings can be collected before they foul the bed. Just as it should become second nature for you to notice abnormalities in each horse's physiology and behaviour, likewise his faeces and urine should be examined daily because they are an indication of whether or not there is anything amiss. Once a routine has been established, nothing, save for activities surrounding the horse (such as a competition), should be allowed to disrupt it; and certainly not human negligence.

No matter how familiar you are with your horse, he should always be warned of your approach to avoid startling him unnecessarily. Use your voice to reassure him for although he may not differentiate between words he will understand their tone. Good stable manners are the foundation of a horse's respect for you which, together with confidence, is the basis of a sound partnership between you. He should be taught to move back from the door as you enter and to stand quietly in his box whilst you attend him. Likewise he must learn to move over when you ask him. Although some people prefer to tie a horse up whenever they are in the box with him there is no reason why he should not be made to respect correct and proper handling at all times. There is nothing more annoying (and often embarrassing) than an ignorant horse who has never been taught any manners, apart from the inconvenience. Naturally one should make allowances when the horse is put under stress, such as at competitions where as a fit horse he is likely to become excitable and behave differently, but even so he ought never be allowed to be rude to you. Discipline should begin at home at an early age.

The actual routine chores for any competition horse who is stabled are, by and large, identical in composition. We have already highlighted the need to be observant and attend to detail in every aspect of horsemanship and no less so in stable management for its contribution to getting a horse fit should never be underestimated.

The barn system of stabling, undoubtedly convenient to work in. It must offer adequate ventilation and a window or door at the back of each box so that the horses can look out.

Mucking out is usually one of the first jobs of the day and may coincide with the first feed. It is assumed that if you are a competitor it won't be necessary to explain how to carry out these basic stable chores, only to remind you of the need to make a thorough job. A clean, deep bed, whether it be straw, shavings, sawdust, peat or shredded newspaper is first of all healthy, and secondly of greater comfort to the horse. Bear in mind that once he is in work he should be encouraged to lie down to rest his legs, although of course he can sleep standing. Once the mucking out and bedding down is complete, this is the best time to tidy the yard and muck-heap. The appearance of the latter is often overlooked but a few minutes spent stacking and treading it down each day will help it to rot better and make it easier to handle with machinery if it has later to be transported. A neat muck-heap is often an indication that the yard has a good standard of stable management. If you are establishing a yard for the first time, make a point of siting the muck-heap at a convenient distance from the yard but not too close to the stables to cause problems with flies during the summer. You may have to allow access for a tractor and trailer or lorry.

The safety aspects of equine welfare and yard management need to be in the back of your mind at all times. Tools and equipment such as wheelbarrows and buckets are potential hazards if the horse has access to them.

Racking up a horse is a simple exercise providing common sense is applied. With any horse, no matter how quiet he is by nature, it is safer to tie him up using a short piece of string between the lead rope or chain and the fixture to which he is to be anchored. If he is startled and as a result pulls back he will then break the string before the headcollar.

Fire routine is something that is not always practised in private yards. Every member of the establishment should know where to locate fire extinguishers and be familiar with the procedure in the event of a fire. That also goes for the horse-box too.

The feed store, fodder and straw barns are also hazardous areas if not maintained with due regard for safety. Vermin are always a problem where food is kept so every effort should be made to deter them by housing sacks off the ground and sweeping the feed shed daily. There is always a risk of vermin contaminating food and of chewing through electrical wire. The latter can result in a fire, perhaps in your absence, so vermin control is well worth the money. As fond as you may be of cats, and yes they do keep the mice down, alas some do tend to foul the hay.

Gutters and drains should be kept free of blockages, the latter being disinfected at least weekly. If your stables are occupied for twelve months of the year it will be necessary to wash the stable floors from time to time because the ammonia in the horses' urine pollutes the atmosphere. However, most yards find time for a spring-clean, when painting and building maintenance is carried out. It is hoped that such tasks as window cleaning, cobwebbing, manger and bucket cleaning are carried out more regularly, i.e. at least once a week.

Still on the subject of safety and maintenance, paddock and arena fencing should obviously be kept in a secure state with no protrusions such as wire or nails to harm the horses.

To many, such basic information regarding safety may seem too elementary to warrant a mention in a text on getting horses fit but we have all heard stories of how negligence has caused a horse to miss a competition through unnecessary injury. Sometimes an animal is side-lined for the rest of a season and hours of careful fitness preparation are wasted. To mention all potentially hazardous items and situations would fill another chapter, so let common sense prevail.

There seems to be a variety of methods of grooming these days and I'm sure some traditional stud grooms would deplore some modern approaches. So many details are overlooked today because we seem to be in so much hurry and this, unfortunately, happens with grooming, clipping and trimming. Far fewer people singe their horses as a means of trimming 'cat hairs' on beards and legs, probably because they are reluctant to use a candle in the absence of a singeing lamp. Although scissors may be quicker, singeing leaves a more natural finish. Undoubtedly clippers make life much easier but the use of an electric grooming machine is a matter of personal preference. Whichever means you use the object remains the same: to clean the horse's coat by removing grease, dust, sweat and mud using a vigorous action which will stimulate the horse's circulation at the same time. If a horse is partly living out he will, of course, need some natural grease in his coat to help protect him from the weather. This is no excuse not to remove sweat thoroughly after he has worked. Good grooming goes hand in hand with a healthy, fit horse for he cannot excrete waste products (in the form of sweat) from his system efficiently if his pores are not kept clean.

It is, of course, for this reason that it is so necessary to clip a competition horse. By expecting him to work whilst he has a full winter coat will not only hinder the fittening process but also be actually harmful to his health. Any condition that he began with can often be lost if the coat is not removed at an early stage of the work programme. Just what type of clip you choose will depend on each horse's individual situation, i.e. the type, intensity and regularity of work, environment, time of year, facilities and to some extent personal preference. To compensate for the loss of natural coat he will need as much rugging as is necessary to maintain normal body temperature without calling on his own energy resources. Again the type of horse will dictate the need for clothing both in the stable and out. A cold-blooded horse who feels the cold as soon as he is undressed will benefit from wearing an exercise sheet or rug on days when it may not seem cold to you and when other horses are comfortable without. He will rely on your discretion and common sense.

The equestrian discipline you choose and your own preference will influence whether or not you pull your horse's mane and tail. Obviously if you have to plait the mane every week it is more convenient if it is pulled short and level. On the other hand, if your horse is a part- or full-bred Arab competing in long-distance rides then his mane and tail would be left in their natural state. Trimming whiskers, ears, etc., does not meet with everyone's approval, though it is fairly safe to say that the majority of show people wouldn't dream of exhibiting their animals without them having been shaved! It is a job which requires patience because many horses resent it, especially if too much hair is pulled at any one time. Every effort should be made to minimise the stress effect on the horse caused by such things as clipping, mane and tail pulling, or any activity which we submit him to for our own benefit. To this end any unnatural experience he is asked to endure should be introduced gradually. We cannot reasonably expect him to tolerate what we so readily take for granted if we fail to give him every chance of understanding.

One of the facets of grooming most relevant to fitness preparation is strapping or banging. This is usually done once the horse has been cleaned and many establishments would not consider the horse groomed if banging was not a feature of their management. To be effective, the groom, using either a hay wisp, leather pad or folded stable rubber, must energetically and rhythmically bang the horse's muscles, i.e. neck, shoulder and quarters, which will cause the horse to flex them. The amount of time taken and emphasis on particular muscles to be toned will depend on the type of work he has to do. Care needs to be taken not to startle a horse who is not used to it and he must be made to stand still and square if he is to benefit properly. It is fair to say that time employed banging a horse contributes to his fitness and it therefore applies to all types of competition horse. Obviously if a horse shows abnormal signs of resistance to it he may have damaged a muscle and veterinary advice should be sought before resuming banging.

Shampooing and washing down is carried out regularly on competition horses other than show stock both at home and at events. Providing the horse is kept plenty warm enough in cold weather and every care taken to prevent him catching a chill there is usually no harm done. Obviously a horse who is not completely healthy must not be washed down. While many traditionalists deplore the practice, no doubt the horse himself finds it invigorating after sweating, especially on a hot day. There is often no better way of cleaning a greasy mane or tail, or of stopping a horse from rubbing. Grooming kits and rugs will need to be washed regularly too because there is no point in trying to groom a horse with dirty kit.

It can been seen in later chapters that the role of the blacksmith and the type of shoes you choose for a specific competition play an all-important part. Blacksmiths are valuable craftsmen and their contribution to your participation in an equestrian sport should never be taken for granted. Always give your blacksmith fair warning whenever possible of your horse's shoeing requirements so that your fitness and competitive schedule is not disrupted as a result of mismanagement on your part. All blacksmiths are busy people but the chances are that if you respect this and do not expect him to attend to your horses at a few hours' notice, then an emergency will be treated as such. Like most business people, the blacksmith has a list of bad debtors; be sure you are not included. Heed his advice with regard to types of shoe, pads and studs, for every horse's requirements are different.

Your veterinary surgeon, too, is a vital member of your 'team'. The horse's health relies heavily on your observation and judgment as to when to call in the vet and when not to waste his time. Your vet is there to advise you on all veterinary matters, routine and otherwise. There is no room for false economy and short cuts when it comes to your horse's welfare. Worming and vaccinations must have a strict programme for each horse. His health and subsequent fitness depend on his being free from worms so be sure to act to prevent rather than cure. It is often a condition of entry for competitions that each horse is vaccinated against flu and that certificates are up to date. Immunisation against tetanus is an obvious necessity and can be combined with the flu injection. Your vet will advise if the horse should be rested after these inoculations. Although there are a few horse dentists in the country, most of us call upon our vet to check teeth. The horse's teeth will normally need rasping about once a year and the importance of seeing that this is carried out should never be overlooked. Several problems and ailments are related to the teeth and if your horse is showing any signs of discomfort, for example with eating or bitting, have his teeth examined immediately.

The care and maintenance of saddlery allows no room for negligence in any sort of stable yard whether or not you are a competitor. Galls and sores caused by dirty or ill-fitting tack are sadly an indication of poor management. No expense should be spared on buying quality saddlery and in keeping it supple and clean. Accidents happen to everyone but they cannot be tolerated if they result from broken saddlery which has not been maintained in good repair. As the tack is cleaned *each day,* care should be taken to examine it for cracks or loose stitches and buckles, especially before a competition. Any equipment that is stored, such as rugging, will need guarding against moths and mice. The temperature of the tack-room is fairly crucial, particularly in the winter when leather is prone to harden if the air is too warm or to develop mould if it is damp. Security, too, is a worry today especially in competition yards where there are often a lot of valuable items. Marking your tack either by indenting your name or postcode is recommended if you are to have any chance of recovering it after a theft.

Whilst still on the subject of stable management it is suggested that those who do not do so already, would find it an advantage to keep a diary in which to include such things as worming dates, blacksmith and vet visits. All veterinary treatment, with notes on any allergies could be recorded, as well as details of each horse's fitness and competition programme. If you have several horses you may need a diary for each horse and someone must be prepared to keep it up to date.

Lastly in this chapter it is felt necessary to mention the importance of communication between those responsible for the day-to-day management of the yard. Suffice it to say that in busy competition yards there is so much to remember, especially once the season has begun and horses and people are coming and going at all hours, that too often a matter is overlooked or a message not conveyed. Perhaps a change in a horse's diet or veterinary treatment is not dealt with promptly simply because of an oversight by someone; after all, we are only human. It is therefore a good idea to use a message board or note pad to ensure that organisation of your stable yard is implemented efficiently.

4 A State of Fitness

In case anyone has any misconceptions about getting a horse fit, it must be stressed from the start that this chapter can only offer guidelines based on experience and case studies. While there are principles to follow for fittening work with horses of each discipline of equestrianism, no two horses are the same in any way. The day-to-day schedule for each horse must be flexible to a degree, allowing for such variables as the weather, time of year, availability of facilities such as an arena and, of course, the general well-being of the horse. Although it is hoped that the foregoing chapters will assist competitors in preparing their horses for competitions, drawing attention to the many incidentals which are all-important in the production of the fit horse, success depends very much on experience. But we must all begin somewhere, whether we are a weekend competitor satisfied with participation or an ambitious rider striving for success in a chosen field. Whichever category you belong to, much of the satisfaction will come from knowing that you have arrived at the competition with a horse or horses who are well prepared both mentally and physically. The purpose should always be to finish a competition with the knowledge that your horse could not have done more without causing himself undue stress and that he did not show any unnecessary signs of fatigue. One of the secrets of fittening a horse is to always work the animal within his capabilities. Whatever the discipline, the horse chosen should have enough quality to be capable of performing his task adequately without ever having to stretch himself to the limit. In other words, a fit horse who can achieve satisfactory results without being pushed into top gear will enjoy a longer competitive career. Remember: it is speed that does the damage to a horse.

The type of horse you choose will depend on many things, but above all the type of discipline in which you are to compete must be the decisive factor. You will then need to establish what the optimum fitness is for the horse, bearing in mind that natural ability as well as type will influence his training programme. It doesn't necessarily follow, though, that he will be less susceptible to injury if he has more quality. Apart from unavoidable accidents, the resistance to injuries of a competition horse will rely a great deal on his preparation.

If the horse has been in a fit condition before, it will invariably be easier to 're-tune' him for another season because physiologically he has adjusted from his natural state. His constitution will harden, too, once he is used to the changes of alternating routine from work to rest over a twelve-month period. Once specific muscles have been built up for a particular use, reconditioning is a matter of tuning rather than developing a part or parts which have never been put under stress before.

Obviously we have to know before we start training how we wish the muscles to develop, whether it be for speed, stamina or strength.

The first time a horse is brought into work, education represents at least half of the exercise period which goes hand in hand with training and therefore fitness. Obviously the older he is the easier he will find it to adapt to a different environment albeit from field to stable. If he is a new member of the yard, being brought straight into work, allowances should be made for the change, especially with the young horse.

Before work can begin on a horse at any stage, he

must first of all be as healthy as possible. All precautions should have been taken with regard to worming, flu and tetanus vaccinations and checking of teeth, and a visit from the blacksmith should have been arranged in good time so that you are not delayed in starting the training programme. One has to be prepared for set-backs in any routine but prevention is better than cure in every case so we should see to it that any interruptions in his progress are not caused by our negligence. Before fitness comes good health and soundness of wind, heart, lungs and limbs, so if your horse has any inherent problems which need treatment these should be sorted out before any

The end of a winter holiday.

harmful stress is put on them. Each horse will react differently to being brought in after his holiday and allowances should be made if he is of a nervous disposition or perhaps misses friends from whom he has been parted. The transition from field to stable for any horse is less drastic if it is done gradually, perhaps by turning out each day reducing the time daily until he has adapted. Dietary changes should be made by degrees, as has been explained in previous chapters. Any sudden alterations can so easily upset the horse's system that he does not utilise his food fully and he may, as a result, lose condition or 'go back' as it is known. From his idle state to one of controlled exercise his conditioning work will go hand in hand with his diet, the principles of which have been explained earlier.

To help assess and monitor fitness throughout a training programme, an intimate knowledge of each horse, including his normal temperature, pulse and respiration, is essential. It is recommended that his TPR rates are taken after training sessions during the whole of the fittening process, recording the time taken for each to return to normal. By so doing we can appreciate and begin to assess the horse's state of fitness at any one time. Abnormalities in TPR rates are, of course, an early indication of ill-health although in many instances they may fluctuate purely as a result of stress.

The longer a horse has been rested, the more slow work he will need at the start of the work schedule. This slow work at the beginning is crucial in many ways. Firstly, his muscles, which have become soft and flabby, will need to be built up gradually so that as they grow in density and strength the tone of them improves considerably. This growth of muscle will need nourishment which is provided by protein in the food. No matter how well toned a muscle is, it is always vulnerable to strain if too much is asked of it, particularly when the horse is cold. During the horse's rest period his muscles will have gone out of shape faster than his skeletal frame, therefore the slow work at the start is an important part of reconditioning his body as a whole.

Microscopic examination has shown that there are two types of muscle fibre: slow twitch and fast twitch. Basically, slow twitch fibres are relatively slow to contract and relax, while fast twitch muscles have faster contraction and relaxation rates. Results of recent research show that by taking a biopsy of a horse's muscle it is possible to establish which type of muscle fibre that horse naturally has, thereby showing to which sport he would be most suited. This can be very useful with racehorses in helping to determine the distance over which a particular horse would be best trained to race.

While the muscles grow in strength and size through gradually increased demand, the circulatory system will become more efficient because its job is to deliver oxygen to the muscles via the heart. During exercise, capillaries expand to accommodate this process in order to keep the muscles supplied with as much blood as possible. We should always be aiming to increase the aerobic (with oxygen) capacity of muscle fibres through the training thereby postponing the formation of lactic acid, the waste product which if allowed to build up can cause muscle cramps and fatigue.

Another function of the circulation is to feed the skin with nutrients. Just how efficiently the system is operating will be seen in the bloom of the coat and the obvious improvement in condition. Blood tests are a useful aid in measuring the state of the horse's fitness as well as supplying various other information which an owner may need. Analysis of the blood can provide, for example, a haemoglobin count; details of sugar levels, nutriments and proteins; and detect the presence of anaemia and parasites. There are several more things which can be discovered in blood tests and your vet will advise you as to which tests your horse needs.

The sedimentation (sediment or waste products) in a horse's blood is another fitness indicator. When a blood sample is taken and left to stand in a container the sediment will fall to the bottom. The fitter the horse is becoming, the more slowly the sediment falls. Also red blood corpuscles increase in number with fitness and consequently there are more newly formed ones at any one time in a fit horse.

The framework or skeleton of the horse is made up of very different types of bone which, like any other part of the horse, need adequate preparation for the increasing strain which is to be put on them. Bones which comprise the limbs should be given every chance to harden by walking the horse on the roads before any faster work is introduced so damage such as sore shins can be safeguarded against. Bones actually respond to exercise by changing their structure, and bones which endure the most stress, for example the bones of the fore-leg, become densest. This in turn strengthens them, increasing their capacity for work. Young horses who are still growing are constantly re-shaping their bone structure and are therefore more vulnerable to damage caused by overstress.

Whilst every part of the horse deserves careful preparation for any athletic performance, tendons and ligaments should always be regarded as delicate structures and given as much protection as practicable. Much of the damage caused to those soft tissues can be blamed on inadequate preparation for the job they are expected to do. Wear and tear on them can often mean that the horse will have to be laid up for long periods. It is therefore prudent (to say the least) that every rider and groom should have a consummate knowledge of their horse's legs, particularly below the knee. Any heat and/or swelling can then be detected at the earliest opportunity and treated promptly. Experience will, of course, help you to judge the severity of any abnormalities but if you are in any doubt at all rest the horse until a professional opinion is sought. There is certainly no room for complacency when it involves a horse's soundness. Risks are not worth taking if you value your horse and his competitive career. Only by familiarising yourself with his idiosyncrasies can you have any hope of saving him from further damage if he is showing signs of strain and give him every chance of recovery before long-term damage threatens his career.

The many physiological changes which occur in the horse will become evident to you through the whole process of conditioning. The effect that fitness has on the horse's temperament is shown in different ways, and much depends on his breed and character. He may become more sensitive and indeed bad-tempered but this is something we have to learn to tolerate and not check unduly. Often his quality of performance will rely on tactful handling and riding, not least when he is put under stress for your enjoyment.

It is recommended that boots or bandages are fitted for protection whenever the horse is being worked, travelled or turned out, especially if his action causes him to hit himself. Young horses who are unbalanced are more susceptible to injuries through weaknesses and allowances should be made, particularly when riding over uneven terrain, to safeguard against them. The use of knee-pads during road work will provide some protection if the horse should stumble. When a horse first comes into work, care should be taken to ensure that tack or clothing does not rub and chafe skin which will be soft. Surgical or methylated spirits will help to harden off the back but care must be taken if the horse has a sensitive skin not to blister it. The corners of the mouth will also be soft and delicate if the horse has not worn a bit for some time. Examine daily and bathe any sore parts with salt water.

The initial walking period that each horse needs before trotting is introduced will depend on many things. The main considerations must be: the discipline in which he is to compete, i.e. the duration and intensity of fitness required; his breed; age; temperament; previous fitness; and period of rest prior to recommencing work. It is obviously easier if you have experience of a previous fittening programme for a particular horse, but no matter what your target the process of walking at the start of each programme has the same benefit if it is carried out correctly. The purpose must be to slowly increase the length of time taken, say, beginning on day one with just twenty minutes and building up appropriately to the type of work required. In the case of a show horse this may only be one hour but an endurance level of fitness will generally require two hours. A casual stroll with the horse off the bit will obviously not benefit him anything like an active, purposeful walk where he is ridden into his bridle. But at the same time he must not be expected to work at any pace too soon and any form of exercise or schooling must be done gradually. Common sense should guide you as to when a horse is ready to take up the bit and for how long each day, so that he is never asked to do too much too soon and risk injury. Whilst training methods will differ from yard to yard, there are some aspects of fittening work that will prevail throughout, such as balance, rhythm, form and flexion. The object must be to develop a supple, responsive and fit athletic horse who is capable of realising his potential comfortably.

Most of us will aim to do most of our walking exercise on the roads. The type of terrain will play a major part in the progress of fitness. Steep hills should obviously be avoided at the beginning of training until the horse is capable of negotiating gradients in both directions without straining himself. Once he is strong enough hill work will be of enormous benefit in developing his fitness providing he is ridden correctly with his head lowered in order to extend and strengthen his back muscles when he is walking uphill. At the same time the weight should be taken off his back by leaning forward out of the saddle and he must be made to walk properly in a straight line without jogging. Whilst hill work is particularly beneficial for endurance-type horses who need to develop

Hill work being correctly executed.

stamina, those animals such as polo ponies, dressage and show horses will not be at a disadvantage if their fitness work is carried out on level terrain. Some horses will need more walking than others before they are sufficiently strong enough to start trotting or any form of schooling.

The type and state of the going will also play their part and while free-draining land is ideal for horses to work on, due consideration must be given throughout the seasons as to the effect it will have on your horse and how he performs. Horses do have preferences with regard to the state of the going and only experience will tell you which your horse prefers. Extreme conditions either way can be harmful if reasonable care is not taken. Deep, muddy going can strain ligaments and tendons while uneven and hard ground is liable to jar up a horse for some time.

Once the horse has done enough walking over a period of weeks, schooling work will begin. It is not intended to detail the many aspects of schooling work in this chapter; equitation is another book. Having said that, it may be necessary at this stage to define that work is when a horse is schooled or educated and is not necessarily sufficient exercise. The effect of exercise on the horse's muscles has been previously explained and as they become more active, so too do all the other vital organs such as the lungs, heart, kidneys and liver. The increased circulation results in more vigorous movements by the respiratory muscles, i.e. chest walls, diaphragm and abdomen, thus the organs of digestion are aided and sluggishness of the bowels or constipation is less likely. Superfluous fat and watery tissues are removed from the body. The volume of the muscles is increased, their elasticity, tone, responsiveness to stimuli, power of contraction and blood supply heightened. The respiratory system is made to accommodate the oxydisation of vastly greater amounts in a shorter space of time than normal. The heart muscle, the main pump of the circulatory system, hypertrophies and the walls of the smaller arteries, the secondary pumps of the circulatory system, are keyed up to the highest state of responsiveness to local requirements. If exercise is neglected and the horse is still fed energy-producing foods — e.g. starch — symptoms of colic, azoturia or lymphangitis are likely to occur. Over exercising is equally harmful especially if the horse is unfit and not in good condition. Excessive exertion results in certain muscles becoming over developed and later wasting away. Overstress on the animal's strength endangers organs as well as structural components and can lead to dilation of the heart, broken wind and roaring to name but a few disasters. It is possible that a horse may suffer a fatal collapse due to heart failure, rupture of a large artery or sheer exhaustion, although death usually occurs through complications.

On achieving optimum condition for any horse it is possible to produce a state of staleness whereby speed and stamina diminishes and the only solution appears to be rest. As a precaution against this many trainers will spend the final week before a major competition such as a three-day event or a 25-mile long-distance ride concentrating on slow work, having given the horse a test about a week before the main goal. By so doing they hope that the horse will arrive at the peak of condition, both physically and mentally fresh. If you cannot confidently adopt this method it is too late to try and improve his condition over a few days. This strategy generally applies to endurance-type horses but it can be seen later, in the show-jumping chapter, how it is adopted for a different form of fitness.

A detailed training plan which incorporates all aspects of fitness and schooling over the months from the day a horse comes in to work up to his first competition is essential. It will be necessary to be flexible throughout the programme making any adjustments which will be found to improve the fittening process for a particular horse. Firstly, a competition schedule, on which a fitness programme is based, will have to be devised. Suppling exercises such as pole work or cavalettis are beneficial to any horse even if he is not expected to jump. They also offer a variety to routine as indeed does lungeing. As with all forms of training though, it must be carried out correctly if the horse is to benefit albeit in the form of exercise. The same goes for long-reining although sadly its contribution to training not just in the young horse is often disregarded. This, however, is not an occupation for the unskilled horseman or -woman but if it does interest you it is recommended that expert guidance is sought.

As with any aspect of fitness it is unrealistic to lay down any hard and fast rule. We must call on experience and common sense, never to do too much too soon and be prepared to learn from our mistakes hoping they have not harmed the horse. Patience is essential with animals and not least when preparing a horse from his raw and natural state. To hurry is to count the cost, only to regret endangering the horse's welfare. Always 'play it by ear' and learn to anticipate the horse's reaction to any question you ask of him. It should always be your intention to keep him happy and contented so that he may enjoy his work. At whatever stage of fitness the horse is in, a little stress and sweating is necessary to increase his capacity for more work but too much is counter-productive. Having prepared a horse to perform adequately without distressing him throughout and after a competition you will at least have some experience on which to base further attempts with different horses. As well as the experience, you will derive enormous satisfaction which will make all the months of hard work very worthwhile.

5 Interval Training

Interval training is a system which has been used by human athletes for more than two decades in their preparation for such sports as athletics, swimming and cycling. Based on physiological experiments it has proved easily adaptable for conditioning horses providing the principles are adhered to. Jack LeGoff, the United States equestrian team trainer, first adopted it for the American three-day event horses and under his guidance they have been using it successfully for several years now. In this country a few trainers of eventers and long-distance horses have tried their own interpretation of the method and whilst the principles may have been followed, many riders insist that their programmes are merely a variation on the same theme. Before any form of fitness preparation can be undertaken we need to know the horse intimately and have a profound understanding of his requirements, capabilities and limitations. Any training programme must, of course, be tailor-made to meet these factors and no less so than when using the method of conditioning endurance-type horses known as Interval Training. Where cantering and galloping sessions are used for eventers, long-distance horses would perhaps be worked at slower paces and they may quantify a routine of interval training in terms of mileage rather than metres per minute. Eventing is, of course, timed over metres per minute so it makes sense to train with this in mind because time is so crucial in the event and the ability to pace your horse over a given distance, on differing terrain, should be learnt at an early stage, so as not to be penalised for going too slowly.

Before a programme of interval training can begin a horse must have completed a certain amount of basic fitness work. Accounting for each horse's requirements we could expect a horse to be no less than six weeks into his training programme, having worked for at least an hour per day doing road work and, for many horses, some flat schooling work. The foundation of any fitness is, of course, based on the depth of a horse's condition. This will rely a lot on the gradual progression of exercise from the outset, so with the confidence that this has been carried out as well as it should have been, you can then devise an interval-training schedule on which the rest of the programme will be based.

Obviously the horse must be sound in every way before he is introduced to interval training. It may, however, prove to be inappropriate for some horses, and it is not recommended for youngsters who are generally insufficiently developed both physically and mentally for such a rigorous routine. In order to establish the best way of training any horse for any discipline, we must appreciate his capabilities and how to achieve the ultimate performance or top yield for that horse without straining him unduly. The success of interval training depends on the implementation of systematic and progressive work, though the degree of effectiveness requires not only experience but also skill on the part of the rider/trainer.

It is probably more scientific than conventional training and for that reason it is not everyone's choice, but for those who are prepared to acknowledge that scientific discoveries have a place in the fittening of competition horses and use this information to the horse's advantage, then interval training is certainly worth looking into. It is not suggested for one moment that it is too scientific in practice and therefore no one should be put off from trying it on those grounds. What is important is for the rider to be prepared to take pulse and respiration rates both during and after each session of fast work. Some people take the horse's temperature, too, immediately after he has recovered from work but this is perhaps not so essential as monitoring the pulse and respiration rates. It is, however, necessary to establish average rates for each horse in a given situation. Allowances must be made for the weather and changes of environment as well as any other situation which places additional stress on a horse. The way he handles each situation will depend on his temperament: an excitable horse will sweat more than one of a placid nature. As a means of evaluating fitness, pulse and respiration rates must be taken at the same points each time if they are to be an accurate assessment of the state of fitness and rate of progress. A horse at rest will normally have a pulse rate of 36−42 beats per minute and during work this may rise to over 200. It is suggested that the optimum work rate should be around 80−150 if the horse is to benefit most from his training. Respiration, which at rest is usually 10−16 breaths per minute, should not go above 100 during work.

As we know, the fitter a horse becomes the faster his recovery from exercise will be. His weight loss as a result of exertion will lessen as he advances in his conditioning work. Therefore weighing him would be another aid to determining his progress, at intervals of, say, a week. Again when monitoring any facet of the horse's state, we must have a starting point. The breeding, sex, condition, and previous training of each horse should also be considered before an interval-training programme can be created. At the same time we need to know just what is required of the horse in terms of the speed over which a specific distance has to be covered, as well as the difficulty, length and intensity of the course. The weather and terrain are critical factors in any training situation and familiarity will help us to make the most of those conditions which best suit the horse.

So how does interval training differ from any other form of training? Basically, the idea is just as the name suggests: a period of specific work followed by a brief interval of rest which is timed so that the horse only partially recovers from his exertion before he is asked to work again. The principle is to develop and subsequently extend his capacity for more intensive work as the training progresses. As always we must avoid overstressing the horse and to be confident of this we must ensure that his work routine is gradual, that we have monitored his pulse and respiration rates, and have a thorough understanding of his capacity throughout the training. Whilst we have to work out an individual routine at the start of each programme we must recognise the need for change at any time. This applies to every horse even if he has used this method before because conditions change and his reaction to those changes may alter as he grows older. The object is to systematically increase the intensity and duration of regulated effort whilst reducing or maintaining the time spent on partial rest intervals. The purpose of allowing the horse only partial recovery from his exertion during these intervals is to encourage the body's organisms to recover whilst the muscular effort is only temporarily reduced. By repeating a series of specific effort we are effectively building up the horse's strength and improving both his respiration and circulation, which as we know increases the aerobic capacity of the muscular system. As his fitness develops so, too, will his resistance to fatigue, something which if we are not careful can have serious effects. What is as important as anything is the frequency with which we ask the horse to perform these series of work-outs. It is suggested that for horses in fast work, i.e. eventers, three or four days a week (every other day) is a suitable guideline because they need the days of slower work in between for their metabolism to return to normal.

Our facilities and the time of year (let alone the weather if we don't have the use of an all-weather track) are probably going to affect us a great deal when deciding on a routine. If we rely on the generosity of farmers allowing us to use their land for galloping work we may

All-weather gallops with a gradual gradient offer ideal facilities for working the eventer at faster paces.

find that our venue will alter and as a consequence gradients may vary. Thus we have to be flexible in the length and speed of any one training session. Obviously we will have to use our common sense and adapt the effect of these variables to suit the horse. Many people will argue that there is no substitute for hill work in preparing the endurance horse and that distances can be reduced at the most by a quarter. It depends on our interpretation of hills and whether we are using rolling hills or steep banks. All these variations make it impossible to lay down any hard and fast rules for fittening horses and show why so much relies on the horseman's instinct.

On the day of an interval-training session we must begin by warming up the horse, firstly by walking, progressing to trotting, until he is suitably supple and prepared for fast work. This can generally be achieved over twenty to thirty minutes. The number of work periods in any one session will depend entirely on your goal and the stage of training but at the beginning three canters would be enough. The rest intervals at the start of the programme are usually three or four minutes to give the horse time to almost recover. The time and speed of each canter will also depend on individual requirements but the duration of each canter is usually between three and six minutes.

If we consider that the training programme for a three-day event horse is usually fifteen weeks, the last six to nine weeks before the three-day event might be taken up with interval training. As a guideline only, the start of an interval training programme may comprise:

    3 minutes canter at 400 metres per minute
    4 minutes rest
    3 minutes canter at 400 mpm
    3 minutes rest
    3 minutes canter at 400 mpm

After the last canter the horse should be gradually cooled down with gentle exercise, including a steady trot, for at least thirty minutes. At the start of the programme this might be as much as an hour but the important thing to remember is not to allow the horse to stand before he has fully recovered from strenuous work and his system has returned to its normal state.

Bearing in mind the principles of interval training, the subsequent sessions must be geared to suit the progress of the particular horse, gradually increasing the work and the speed of the canters whilst decreasing or maintaining the rest intervals. Eventers may build up the speed of the canters to around 550 mpm and, ultimately, say, on the final canter of the last two sessions before the event, to 690 mpm (steeplechase speed). There are numerous variations on the time spent on each interval and some may choose to split a session into perhaps:

> 4 minutes at 400 mpm
> 3 minutes walking
> 5 minutes at 550 mpm
> 1 minute at 600 mpm
> 2 minutes walking
> 3 minutes at 400 mpm
> 1 minute at 550 mpm
> 1 minute at 400 mpm
> 1 minute at 690 mpm

Most of the canter work should be carried out at about half speed with the increase in pace only coming towards the end of the programme. Remember that it is the fast speed which so often is the cause of damage to limbs. The distance your horse will cover in the time is obviously relative to the terrain and ground conditions but, again, if you are measuring the work in terms of mileage, these factors and any others relative to your calculations must be taken into account. The figures mentioned are, after all, *only an example,* designed purely to give some idea of how a timetable is formulated. Theory is no substitute for practice where horses are concerned and only you will know how to devise a training programme for your horse (or hopefully you will do by the time you have read this book).

The days in between interval-training sessions may be spent doing road work and schooling on the flat and over fences, again depending on your goal. Eventers will usually require one and a half to two hours' work per day on these days if they are to establish the necessary depth to their fitness. Long-distance riding horses, on the other hand, do not require the same amount of canter work at faster speeds and you may therefore choose to cover a specific number of miles per day at slower paces so that every day might involve a type of interval training.

An example of an interval training type of programme is given in their long-distance riding chapter where Pam James' training schedule for a particular horse is catalogued. Likewise in the eventing chapter, Virginia Holgate offers her own particular version for her three-day event horses. It is interesting to note, though, that since these examples were recorded, both of these riders have made adjustments to their programmes for the same horses although their goals have remained similar; the horses' reactions have changed as well as the conditions in which they are worked. Whilst interval training no doubt has a place in the preparation of horses for endurance events, its success, like any training, will depend on the skill of the trainer and his ability not only to design an ideal programme for each horse but also to recognise the need to change any facet without hindering the horse's progress.

6 Competing

Before arriving at a competition there are several formalities to attend to besides the detailed organisation and preparation required for each horse. Virtually every type of class has its own conditions of entry whether or not it is an affiliated competition. It is therefore up to you to contact the show secretary to ensure that you are familiar with those conditions and any rules which prevail, before you submit your entry. Unaffiliated competitions, i.e. those which are not run under the jurisdiction of the governing body for that particular discipline, do not usually follow the same levels of grading and qualification but there is normally a limit regarding the horse's winnings, otherwise it would be unfair on the owner of a novice horse who is entered in the same class as an experienced campaigner.

Whichever sport or sports you plan to compete in, you will need to plan a schedule of events. It has been suggested in the previous chapter that you have an outline of the competition season at the very start of each horse's fitness programme to enable you to work back from the first event or show. All manner of mishaps can upset your plan but it is essential to organise your season in theory from the beginning.

In order to formulate your plans you must be clear in your own mind just what your ambitions are with a particular horse. Economics do play a major part in the pursuance of those ambitions and for most of us our competitive involvement is dictated by the availability of funds. Even those more fortunate competitors who are commercially sponsored do not always have a completely free rein but are sometimes limited as to how much they do with each horse who is covered by a particular contract. On the other hand, if money is no object, care should be taken not to compete too much with any horse even though he is fit and healthy because he cannot maintain optimum performance indefinitely and you run the risk of overstressing him both physically and mentally. Your budget will need to account for every element which competing involves. For example: registration; membership, travelling (not forgetting the running costs of a vehicle); accommodation and overnight stabling if applicable; and any extra equipment that is needed for both horse and rider.

If you are new to a particular sport it is in your best interests to have studied it thoroughly and to be fully aware of what it involves, both in terms of the type of fitness required of the horse and the rider's ability. All too often the glamorous image portrayed through television attracts enthusiastic young riders who have overlooked the importance of careful preparation of the horse and rely on his ability and generous nature to carry them through. This applies particularly to showjumping although eventing and long-distance riding are now enjoying more popularity than ever before and the quality of fitness is even more crucial for these endurance events. There is nothing unhealthy about modelling oneself on a 'star competitor' – most enthusiastic riders have done so at some stage during their career – but to take short cuts in order to achieve immediate results is risking the horse's soundness and long-term prospects. Utter dedication to the horse and self-discipline are vital prerequisites for a competitor. You must be prepared to commit yourself unselfishly to all that is involved with competing, no matter what level you and your horse are at.

There can be no doubt that sport helps to develop character but only experience can teach you to control and channel your emotions to your advantage during a competitive situation. The temperament of the rider will affect his partnership with each horse. Whereas some combinations are a success it is commonplace to hear of a rider not getting on with a particular horse. Obviously his skills as a horseman will make up for some inadequacies but ability will not always overcome a clash of personalities between horse and rider. As a conscientious horseman/woman you should always be concerned with the day-to-day details of stable management which are so important to the success of any partnership, even if you are fortunate enough to employ a groom.

A novice competitor will sensibly use his first season of competitions to familiarise himself with the horse and its performance and the many aspects of competition life. It will take time and experience to accustom oneself to the various procedures and rules of any discipline of equestrianism which do vary at different levels within those sports. There is never room for complacency either, because even an experienced competitor can make mistakes such as riding the wrong side of a flag or accepting outside assistance when it is forbidden.

No matter how competitive you are at your chosen sport it should be remembered that it is not the winning but the taking part that counts. Having said that, though, it is more important for some people to win than others especially if their livelihood depends on successes in the ring. In some ways commercialism is a very good thing for sport but where animals are concerned the attraction of large prize money can sometimes outweigh due consideration for the horse's welfare. It is hoped that that only happens in exceptional circumstances but often a decision has to be made as to whether or not to run a horse on extreme ground conditions. As far as the author is concerned it is *never* worth risking the horse's soundness for a single effort if there is any doubt whatsoever in your mind and the final decision is yours. Remember, there is always another day. On the other hand, if you are competing as a team member, you may well be instructed to ride where you would otherwise not do so as an individual. For most of us though, it will save a lot of wasted time and effort if you ring the show secretary or perhaps a friend who lives in the locality of the competition, to enquire as to the state of the going before you leave home. Of course, the going can change during the day and you may have to decide once you have arrived, but this is one of the many situations which make every event so different and challenging. It is easier to enter competitions where you have competed before and are therefore familiar with the terrain, the type of going which normally prevails at a particular time of year and the many other aspects which affect the quality of that competition.

Each discipline places its own demands on both horse and rider, affecting each horse differently. Much depends on the horse's own ability and capacity to withstand the rigours of training and competitions. Having gone through months of preparation you will have established a partnership with your horse on which much of the success of your competitive pursuits will rely. Only by familiarising yourself with a horse's idiosyncrasies once he is fit and competing will you be able to judge just which conditions suit him best and how he handles repetitive stress situations thus enabling you to bring out the best of him using your skills as a horseman/woman. Half of the challenge of competing lies in overcoming the problems which are met during the training of each horse; indeed competing would become very dull if a horse performed well every time. No amount of theory can substitute for practical experience in any sport especially where horses are concerned.

Before entering for an affiliated competition you and your horse will have to be registered with the governing body of that equestrian discipline (see Appendix). Once you become a member you will be advised as to which competitions you are eligible for so that you can then go ahead and plan your season. If you have not competed before at the level of a particular discipline in which you are now entering there is much to familiarise yourself with in terms of qualifying, conditions of entry, etc. If a vaccination certificate is required be sure that it is up to date otherwise you could be disqualified; the same goes for the horse's passport, although this is usually only needed at an advanced level. Vaccination against equine influenza is becoming a formality with most disciplines now and it is up to you to check with the relevant organisation or show secretary in good time.

As efficient as you may be in carefully planning your competitions and organising the routine for horses and helpers there will always be the unforeseen disappointments which are beyond anyone's control, such as adverse weather causing the abandonment of an event. With the increased popularity of sports like eventing there is the constant risk of being ballotted out which, if it happens a few times, can be very frustrating. It is therefore wise to enter for some other competition during that same week so that your training schedule is not disrupted for any length of time. This is in fact a double safeguard because you may find nearer the time that your horse is not ready for a particular competition. If so, be sure that any withdrawals are made in good time otherwise you will encounter the wrath of the show secretary (or worse). You will have to learn to endure any disappointments of which the horse may be the cause, such as unsoundness or ill-health prior to an outing. These are all part of the ups and downs of the sport which you have to learn to accept (but which are made easier if you have another horse to ride).

Prior to the actual day of competition, arrangements will have to be co-ordinated with everyone concerned so that you will be able to concentrate on your riding, with the knowledge that your 'team' knows the routine. The day before, it is usually possible and indeed more practical to prepare and load into the vehicle much of the equipment. This avoids any last-minute panic and allows you to check every item for safety as well as utility. This applies particularly to saddlery and any spares which may not have been used since the previous competition. You should also make sure at home that any spare tack does actually fit the horse; don't rely on the leather punch to make adjustments at the last minute on the day. Also check your own equipment as well as the horse's because it is too easy to forget that your jacket is short of a button or that you're using your last hair-net. There are so many items to remember that it is well worth keeping lists; even the most travelled competitor can forget things. Be prepared for every eventuality, especially if you are staying away overnight – apart from the extra equipment needed for the horse there is your own kit such as cooking and bedding items. You may find that the temporary stabling provided needs some structural adjustments by yourself to ensure your horse is comfortable. It is for such emergencies that you should be prepared and carry with you such things as waterproof sheeting, string, and a tool kit which includes nails and staples, wire cutters and wire. Someone must be responsible for ensuring that nothing that might be needed is left at home because it is always easy to blame someone else if there are a few people involved. Keep lists for, say, travelling kit, tack, veterinary kit, feed list and working kit. Make sure each is checked during loading and nothing is left to chance; you can then concentrate on the journey and look forward to the competition with confidence.

Depending on when you leave for a competition your horse will preferably have been fed at least an hour before the journey. Travelling a horse, no matter what the distance or the type of vehicle being used, requires patient care and common sense. One careless accident caused by mishandling can impair a horse's confidence permanently, whether occasioned by loading or during transit. There are several things to consider when travelling horses because ignorance on the part of the driver can create serious stressful situations which often cause the horse to lose condition (which has taken months to establish) before he has actually arrived at a competition. Cornering and braking should be executed as if your cargo were crates of eggs. It would surprise many inexperienced drivers of horse transport just how much a journey can take out of horses if they are not given a smooth ride with every possible chance of balancing themselves. Obviously the longer the distance the more strain on the horse so it is up to you to ensure his journey is made as comfortable as possible if he is to arrive at the competition calm and ready for work.

Safety must always be uppermost in your mind and every precaution taken to ensure that the transporter, whether lorry or trailer, is structurally sound, especially the floor-boards. The roof should be waterproof and indeed high enough for the horse's comfort. Often an animal is reluctant to load if he feels he does not have enough head-room; and poll damage can be serious. Good ventilation, but not draughts, must be provided and this should be checked before *each* journey because every trip is different in terms of the weather and the state of the horse. How each horse is tied for a journey may depend on the animal and the partitions in the transporter but, above all, safety must come first, with every care taken to guard against the many hazardous situations in which a horse can find himself through the owner's negligence.

Generally speaking, for a competition which is near enough to enable you to travel both ways in one day and providing the horse has had access to water before the journey, it is not usually necessary to stop and water. It is a matter of preference, depending on the type of competition involved, as to whether the horse travels with a hay-net.

However, it is certainly not recommended for horses who are to participate in an endurance event such as eventing or long-distance riding, just as one would not give them hay at home before prolonged exercise. Feeding after your class before the return journey is again a matter of preference for each horse. Some will not eat at all until after the journey and there are animals who tend to get colic more easily than others, so beware. If in doubt give your horse a hay-net and wait until you get home before feeding.

Even if your horse displays endless stamina for travelling and competing it will place a certain amount of both mental and physical stress on him which will compound over a season. Repetitive competitive stress probably takes its toll more on show jumpers than on any other horses. Having said that, the eventing seasons are expanding more each year with a briefer respite during the summer than ever before. For this reason your plans for both the spring and autumn eventing season should allow for enough holiday in between to suit the individual horse. Don't expect him to retain his fitness from March to October without adequate rest and recuperation from each season. It will be seen in Chapter 7 that some dressage horses are kept 'ticking over' throughout a twelve-month period so that muscles do not lose their tone completely but then due compensation has to be made to prevent the horse becoming stale during that time.

On the day of a competition all your preparation and detailed organisation will be tested, often down to the last second in some cases. Any oversight on the part of your 'team' will have to be put down to experience and if it means borrowing a sweat-scraper or a pair of spurs from a friend you will see the wisdom of keeping and checking lists. It would seem difficult to forget to load a horse but it has been done before, much to the horror of one driver who discovered the fact when, nearly 100 miles from his yard en route to Switzerland, he stopped at a service station on the M1 and found that he had only four horses instead of five and a ferry to catch. (Although the author was present at the time she disclaims any responsibility.) So check and check again is the message.

Once you have arrived at the venue see that the horse is comfortable, changing any rugging as necessary if the horse is not being tacked up, and have your equipment prepared, i.e. tack and studs etc. It is risking injury to stud the horse up whilst he has to stand in the lorry but if your stud holes have been prepared at home and stoppers or oiled cotton wool fitted it should only take minutes to stud-up when the horse is unloaded. If you have to find the show secretary to collect numbers and declare your intention to run be sure this is done as soon as possible. If you have a course to walk you should have allowed plenty of time for this and located the course map before you set off. Show-jumpers may have to wait for one class to finish before their course is ready to walk. Dressage people have probably the easiest routine of all, because they can ring the show secretary a day or so in advance to find out their times. Showing on the other hand is a much more drawn out affair with classes

This is perhaps the most common stud for hind shoe, for use in good to soft going. With all studs, beware of the horse treading on your foot.

Hand-made, wedge-shaped stud for a hind shoe, used particularly on hard ground; useful for jumping and dressage.

This is an ice stud, again for a hind shoe, for use on very hard, level ground. Generally employed for dressage and show-jumping but not usually for cross country.

This is a front shoe stud, most commonly used in good to soft going, for general competition use. It should be said, though, that many people do not agree with the fitting of front studs and care should be taken when using them.

often running behind schedule; despite gallant efforts on the part of the organisers, something always seems to upset their programme. It is therefore wise if you are showing to find out as soon as you arrive if the classes are running on time, even before you tack up or harness your horse.

If the competition is very local and the horse will not have to stand for long in the lorry or trailer after you arrive you may choose to tack up before you leave home. For any travelling distance, though, the horse must be well protected from possible injury or rubbing. The type of rugging will obviously depend on the horse and the weather and may have to be changed during transit, so be prepared for all conditions.

If you have an interval between classes there may be time to let the horse graze or even eat a small feed, whilst giving you and your helpers a chance to do odd jobs. If you have remembered your tack-cleaning kit take advantage of any spare moment to keep on top of these chores which may save you time later on. The transporter should be mucked out as and when necessary, taking care not to litter the field with straw, always a sore point with organisers.

Once you have finished riding, the horse should be washed down or groomed and suitably rugged before being prepared for travelling. Make sure that not only is he dry but also that his respiration is normal before he is loaded. In conditions of extreme heat and/or humidity your horse will benefit from being washed down between classes if there is time and again depending on the type of competition. Do not, however, allow him large quantities of drinking water at any one time if he is hot or distressed; small sips at frequent intervals are safer. Remember hot-blooded horses sweat more than cold-blooded animals and sweating for long periods of time, e.g. in hot weather during endurance competitions, causes a loss of body weight.

At some events you have to return your number at the end of the day but this won't be as difficult to remember if you had to leave a deposit for it. At all times when you are competing be courteous to the organisers and officials because it is thanks to them giving their time so generously to the sport, often in inclement weather, that the competition is possible. Likewise, they rely on your co-operation and time-keeping for the smooth running of the classes. If you have been stabled away from home during a competition, be sure to leave the stables as you found them. You don't want to acquire a bad reputation as a competitor no matter how successful you become.

PART TWO

7 Dressage

Patricia Gardiner

Patricia Gardiner found herself specialising in dressage sooner than she had planned. In 1967 whilst eventing at Wylye she took a nasty fall which broke both her legs badly. During her period of recovery (which took two years and has in fact still left her unsound), she lost the ride on Welton Gameful, on whom she had planned to compete at Badminton. In 1970 Tricia decided to turn her attention to dressage.

Her involvement with the Three Counties Dressage Group whilst she was living in Herefordshire, together with guidance from Lorna Johnstone, gave her valuable experience which she was then to build on with the help of Robert Hall. He encouraged her to train Manifesto, her home-bred horse whom Robert considered to have great potential.

Lorna Johnstone was to have a permanent influence on Tricia's dressage career. By offering her rides on some advanced dressage horses, which included the chance to ride El Faruco at the Horse of the Year Show and in the Montreal Olympic Games Trial, her ambitions were channelled in the right direction from the beginning. It is, therefore, no surprise to see Mrs P. Gardiner ranked amongst the leading dressage riders in the country today, affectionately regarded as one of the 'dressage queens'. Having competed in a variety of equestrian disciplines all her life she admits that no other riding sport appeals to her in the way that dressage does. The challenge presented by constantly seeking to achieve perfect harmony with different horses as they progress up the ladder, to ultimately reach Grand Prix level after years of dedicated training, is Tricia's *raison d'être*.

Although Tricia is without a novice horse, she does have three horses working at advanced or Grand Prix level. The type of horse she looks for is similar to that which is preferred by eventing people. A show horse who catches the eye as it points its toes ostentatiously

Patricia Gardiner schooling at home. Regular work in the arena develops the proper muscles when carried out correctly – the rider's expression speaks volumes!

does not necessarily have the type of action in his hind limbs and the natural athleticism which is required of the dressage horse. Basic good conformation is just as important for dressage as for any other discipline because any weaknesses caused by bad conformation will eventually manifest themselves as the physical demand upon them increases.

As far as rider fitness is concerned, Tricia believes that in order to do justice to the horse, the rider should do some form of physical training, e.g. swimming, jogging, aerobics or simple stretching exercises to keep the body supple. Stiffness in the rider is immediately transmitted to the horse, resulting in the partnership working in opposition. As with all forms of equestrianism, complete co-ordination is a basic requirement. Stiffness in the rider makes it very difficult or even impossible for the horse to use its body in an athletic, elastic way.

Riding only one horse regularly is a distinct disadvantage to any serious competitor. Faults in a partnership are often not so apparent until the rider gets on another horse, and rider errors can sometimes result in weeks of counter-productive work. This is why most successful riders ride more than one horse a day fairly regularly and have someone to help advise them on the way a horse is going. Furthermore an expereinced rider on your horse will invariably notice any bad habits that are developing.

Riding an experienced horse offers the rider an opportunity to concentrate on his or her position without worrying too much about how the horse is going. Another useful teaching exercise for both horse and rider is lungeing.

The stables at Tricia's home in north Wiltshire are part of a barn system, which she believes is the ideal way of stabling horses. They are usually warm in the winter and cool in the summer because they have enough ventilation without being draughty. Windows at the rear of each box enable the horses to look out, and a central passageway divides the stables down the barn so that horses can be tied up there to be groomed.

On her ten acres of land Tricia has built a sand and plastic arena measuring 60m × 20m which allows her to work the horses on good going all the year round. All the land is level and particularly well drained because of the loamy soil. This also means that the horses can be turned out throughout the year which would not be practical on a clay-type soil. Adjacent to the yard and sand arena are four paddocks which are divided by Flexafence, a type of plastic strip which has proved safer than alternative fencing. Horses are less likely to rub against it or to chew it as they so often do with wood.

The day-to-day care of Tricia's competition horses is in the hands of a girl groom whose daily routine begins with feeding at 7 a.m. If a horse is to be ridden at this time he is fed on his return to the stable. The daily riding programme is varied so that the horses learn to be adaptable at competitions and do not resent being asked to perform at different times of the day. Consequently feeding times have to be adjusted accordingly but normally at home lunch is given as near to 12 o'clock as possible. Tea and supper are fed at 5 p.m. and 8.30 p.m. respectively. Hay is taken away from the horses an hour before they are ridden. Usually all the horses are fed on meadow hay supplied by a neighbouring farmer. Any horse who has a respiratory problem or a cough is fed on Propack, a pre-packed grass which is made along the same lines as silage and is completely dust-free.

All the bedding is made up of deep shavings built on a foundation of hammered chalk, which makes them extremely free-draining. Thus there is never an accumulation of wet shavings which is otherwise difficult to avoid on a concrete floor. Droppings are skepped-out frequently not only to keep the beds clean but also to prevent any dung from collecting in the horses' hooves which could lead to diseases such as thrush.

Tricia is very keen on using a rotary-brush grooming machine because she feels that 'it is an energy-saving way of keeping a coat really clean'. Combined with correct feeding and regular changes of a cotton sheet underneath the rugs, the horses' coats are kept as clean as they can be. Manes and tails are shampooed weekly and in the warm summer months the horses are washed down after work. Clipping is done at any time of the year it is felt necessary, no matter whether it is to remove the summer or winter coat. However, in the autumn each horse is given a trace-high clip, leaving the coat on the back for the worst of the winter months. The last winter clipping removes the coat completely so that there are no clip lines showing when the new coat comes through.

The working year of these dressage horses is unlike that of other competition horses. They do not actually have a long holiday completely roughed off but are kept ticking over for twelve months of the year, having just a few days' holiday now and then whenever necessary or convenient. Even during the close-season the horses are gently hacked or lunged in order to keep their muscles in tune. Tricia explains that as they get older, if they are not ridden for several weeks their muscles would then take months to regain the hard condition that is essential for this type of training. However, if a horse had had a particularly busy schedule of classes he would be rested for a week, during which time he would be turned out daily. As a matter of routine all the horses are turned out after work, weather permitting, which allows them to relax mentally each day. It has been pointed out in an earlier chapter that we should be aiming to keep horses as closely as possible to their natural lifestyle. For this

The use of a mirror enables the rider to watch the horse's quarters whilst performing a half pass.

reason the therapeutic value of turning out daily cannot be over-emphasised.

The horses' training/fitness programme is mainly carried out in the sand arena for periods of thirty to forty minutes. Systematic intensive work is essential for the improvement and advancement of each individual. A session of loose jumping from time to time keeps a horse supple and encourages him to use himself properly without the rider's weight; it also adds variety to his work routine. Hacking around the country lanes is either done after work in the arena or instead of it.

Emphasis is placed on the art and subsequent benefits

of correctly executed lungeing work, which Tricia usually carries out herself. Side-reins are fitted from the bit to the girth, and a cavesson over the bridle enables the lunge line to be attached independently. Lungeing as a form of training lasts for anything up to forty minutes depending on whether or not the horse is to be ridden afterwards. He may even be lunged instead of ridden for several days for different reasons, perhaps because of stiffness. Although all the youngsters are taught to jump in case they do not make the required grade as a dressage horse, none of them are hunted because of the risk of them leaning on their forehand. This, of course, would be a serious fault in the dressage horse who has to learn self-carriage.

Tricia is keen to point out that the horses' routine must be flexible because of the irregular nature of the competition season. As a consequence their day off each week will vary according to when and where a competition is held.

It can be seen that the type of fitness required for a dressage horse can be achieved entirely by working in an arena because Tricia's horses do not do road work as such as part of their fitness programme. At the same time, though, if one is working entirely in the arena due care must be taken not to strain muscles through overworking them in a confined space before they are sufficiently toned. By restricting the horse with the rider's hand through the reins one is more likely to damage muscles which must be supple and free in order to perform movements in an athletic manner. A free forward movement must not be hindered in any way and any stiffness in the rider's hands and shoulders instantly transmits tension to the horse and can lead to overstress of muscles. It should always be remembered that 'collection is impulsion, created and controlled'. This cannot be achieved correctly without suppleness and flexibility. Therefore if a rider has any doubts about the degree of suppleness in a collected horse it is advisable to encourage him to relax on a long rein for a time to enable him to rest muscles which are perhaps tired or unaccustomed to a particular movement.

From time to time Tricia's dressage horses are given a canter round a suitable field as a mental and physical change from the demands of collected work in the school. Galloping is not a necessary part of the dressage horse's training, but a steady canter can improve respiration.

Apart from the use of whip and spurs, artificial aids, e.g. martingales, are not used in Tricia's yard. A thick eggbutt snaffle and flash nose-band compose the standard bridle used at home, although all the horses have to learn to work satisfactorily in a double bridle in preparation for competitions. The correct fitting of the bit is of paramount importance because the horse must be comfortable whilst he is working on a contact with the rider.

Each horse's feeding requirements are given individual attention – an example that no matter what type of fitness you are working towards you must choose a separate diet for each animal, even though the intensity and duration of work may be almost identical, as in the case of dressage horses. Unlike horses in fast work, the dressage horse should be large and round in condition, similar to the show horse. Oats, sugar-beet, micronised barley (this is whole barley which has been rolled and heat-treated to clean it), linseed and boiled barley are the staple diet of all Tricia's horses. The quantities, of course, vary according to the type of animal, its work and the time of year. A dessertspoonful of salt is added to one feed each day for those horses who are in hard work, but every horse has a mineral/salt block permanently in the stable. Any horses, particularly the young sters, who do not need food that is 'heating' have their oats replaced by horse and pony cubes. Barley is boiled daily for any horses who tend to lose condition easily. Twice a week linseed is boiled and subsequently added to the normal evening feeds. Bran is not used regularly, neither is it considered necessary to feed bran mashes. The horses do, however, have daily access to grass, which apart from its nutritive value also acts as a laxative.

Hay is fed three times a day; the majority being at night with only a small net given in the morning before work. The amount of hay varies according to each horse's particular requirements, bearing in mind that the quality and quantity of the daily grass ration will affect the animal's appetite for hay. Vacuum-packed grass, e.g. Propack, replaces conventional hay if it is found that a horse is suffering from an allergy.

Dressage competitions in this country begin in March and end in September, or October for horses who have qualified for the Horse of the Year Show. Planning a routine for the day of a competition is relatively easy for the dressage horse because the rider will know the times for his tests a day or two before the class. If they are to travel on the same day as they are to compete, Tricia's horses are fed at least an hour before they leave home and are given a hay-net for the journey. The travelling time is usually scheduled so that they arrive at least an hour before the class begins. As soon as they arrive the hay-net is removed. The mid-day feed is given whenever practicable, ensuring enough time for the horse to digest it properly before he has to work again. Once the horse has finished work for the day he is offered a hay-net for the return journey. When the horses arrive home and after they have been made comfortable, they are given a small feed if, as is usual, the following day is to be a rest day. Where a competition is a long way from home and lasts for more than one day, the journey is made the day before so that the horses have a chance to rest and settle in to a strange environment.

Generally speaking, competitions in this country are performed on grass and, owing to the peculiarities of our weather, the arenas often tend to be either hard and slippery or muddy and deep. Studs, therefore, play an important role, their size and shape depending on the going at the time. Normally they are fitted in the hind shoes although, occasionally, in extreme ground conditions, they might also be fitted in front as well.

Tricia is particularly selective about the type of shoes her horses wear and she is fortunate enough to have a blacksmith who keeps abreast of current trends by participating in farriery competitions. Consequently he is sympathetic to the requirements of the modern dressage horse and the need for changes in the type of shoes used in competition. Tricia buys her horses' shoes from Italy because she prefers an aluminium type which have a larger bearing surface than those found in this country. Because so little actual road work is done by these horses, their shoes last for up to five or six months. Road studs are fitted behind on all Tricia's horses, and in the summer, leather pads may be worn in the front shoes as a precaution against concussion. The trouble that is taken with the fitting of shoes for these dressage horses reminds us that we cannot pay too much attention to detail if we are to succeed at our chosen sport.

Actually getting the horse fit is one thing but the secret of success lies in turning over every stone to ensure that each facet of the horse's welfare is given equal consideration.

8 Show-Jumping

Peter Robeson

The difference between show-jumping today and that of the fifties and sixties, has perhaps been influential in some ways in attracting a different type of rider. The commercial and professional attitude to what has now been given a more glamorous image, largely due to television coverage, would not have been dreamed of when Peter Robeson began competing. Indeed his approach to this discipline is, and has always been, that of the true amateur. His ideals are, by today's standards, very refreshing, but unfortunately they may not be fully appreciated by many modern young riders who look for short-term success and immediate results as opposed to taking time and patience to develop the art of the sport.

If your priorities lie in producing sound, fit, confident and contented show-jumpers who clearly enjoy and will, with due respect for their limitations, continue to enjoy their competitive life to its fullest potential, then Peter's vast knowledge and craftsmanship will be of interest to you. His understanding of the horse is reflected in his successes over forty-eight years of competing at all levels of the sport. The best qualities of horsemanship and those of a jockey are rarely found in one person but Peter has artistically combined the two. He has the ideal

Peter Robeson competing at Montreal in his second Olympics – he
made his first Olympic appearance in Tokyo, twelve years earlier.
(Leslie Lane)

temperament for someone involved with animals and
has proved over many years of producing horses for
show-jumping that patience is a virtue and will be duly

rewarded. The sport first appealed to Peter at the early age of seven because he felt there were more competitions in show-jumping per year to test the rider's training skills than there were in endurance-type disciplines. Also, with appropriate care the horses generally lasted longer and could be competing up to eighteen years of age.

The show-jumping circuit today places riders and horses under more pressure than ever before. You are required to qualify now for most of the big classes and because of the growth of the sport a computer is used to handle all the information regarding grading, registering and winnings. The points system used by the governing body (the British Show Jumping Association) dictates which competitions you can enter once you are up-graded. If you are ambitious and want to try and keep up with the professionals then you will need two teams (or 'strings' as they are referred to) of horses because there are two seasons which occupy the whole year, i.e. May to October, and October to April. Qualifying is far more important now and in order to meet the requirements you have to be prepared to compete much more than you used to. The idea of having two groups of horses on the circuit means that each horse can be rested within its schedule of competitions whilst you still have other horses at various levels to keep you mounted.

On the whole a far better quality of horse is now sought for show-jumping and in fact Peter prefers Thoroughbreds. The breeds and types vary so much throughout the world that it would be unrealistic to suggest an ideal stamp of horse to look for. Many people argue that mares are more temperamental than geldings but Peter has found in his experience that they are usually quite equal, indeed he has come across a number of geldings who have had a great deal of temperament. He suggests that this criticism of mares is an old wives' tale that will persist.

As a farmer Peter is able to set aside some land for the horses, which fits into the crop rotation. About twenty acres provides the horses with grazing paddocks and enough seed hay. Part of the land is permanent meadow pasture which runs alongside the River Ouse and provides a range of grasses and herbage which cannot be found in leys and offers some of the best forage for horses that nature can provide. Whenever possible all the horses are turned out in a small paddock after their work each day. Although Peter does not feed haylage he suggests that it probably simplifies feeding for those horse owners who are not rural people with an inbred understanding of nutrition and animal husbandry, because of its relative simplicity. Haylage, like all natural foodstuffs, is subject to variation and consequently it is necessary to stick to a 'good average' as a guideline. In some yards it is being fed quite satisfactorily to horses who are out of work but unless you are harvesting the grass yourself there is no surety of which cut you are feeding. The first cut will invariably be high in protein while the feed value in the second and third cuts could be halved. The arable side of the farm provides Peter's horses with all the wheat straw and hay they need, but the concentrates have to be bought in from local feed merchants. Hay is fed in two portions, one in the morning after exercise and the other in the evening.

Peter's feeding methods have always been based on traditional feedstuffs, given according to a strict feed chart, three or four times a day depending on the horses' requirements. The main ingredients of all his feeds are oats, bran and chaff. Steamed oats are fed in conjunction with crushed oats, and only occasionally, when a horse is underweight, will boiled barley be given. Cod-liver oil, seaweed and salt licks are the only additives to this basic diet. As a general rule, all the horses are fed a linseed mash in the evening feed before their day off once a week. On their rest day they are either turned out or, if the weather is inclement, led out in hand for a graze, taking care that they are warm enough and if necessary using a waterproof or New Zealand rug for protection.

As part of the daily grooming routine each horse is strapped or 'banged' with a hay wisp on the neck, shoulders, quarters and loins for about twenty minutes each day. This encourages the right muscles to develop.

Peter and Renée Robeson have lived and farmed in Buckinghamshire for many years and in Peter's heyday their twelve boxes were always full of show-jumpers ranging from novice four-year-olds to teenage Grade As or international horses. Since their marriage the Robesons' show-jumpers have mostly been home-bred. However, and sadly for the show-jumping world, Peter now confines his competition entries to local shows, no longer entertaining spectators with his unique style. Since his British team debut in 1949 riding Craven A, Peter has produced countless horses and has clocked up so many hundreds of competitive miles, he now feels that the time has come to slow down. Fortunately for us, though, he is happy to impart some of his experience and the principles on which his successes were based.

His horses begin their education as yearlings and are long-reined in preference to being lunged. (Peter admits that he has never been keen on lungeing). The initial breaking-in period may only last a couple of weeks, just enough to introduce them to the rudiments of long-reining and to back them with a very lightweight jockey. Each year thereafter, until the horse is physically strong enough and mentally prepared to go into full work, they are long-reined around the farm and country lanes for two or three weeks as well as being lightly ridden at the walk. Peter feels that on the whole, horses are not long-reined anything like as much as they can and should be. Much can be achieved if it is done properly but, as with any schooling method, not everyone is capable of educating a horse in this way. In some aspects a high standard of horsemanship is necessary for long-reining and the trainer needs to have particularly sensitive and careful hands. Anticipation – being able to think extra far ahead of any movements or changes of direction (intentional or otherwise) – is crucial. It is not recommended that novice equestrians should set about long-reining without expert guidance. Once competent, however, it will be found that apart from developing brakes and steering whilst mouthing the horse, it is also possible to establish confidence and consequently courage by teaching the horse to deal with unfamiliar situations and explore new sights and sounds without relying on a companion to lead the way. Poles and cavalettis can also be negotiated so that when the horse is ready to be backed he will be able to concentrate better on carrying a weight and become used to the many new questions that a rider will present rather than having to cope with everything at once.

Long-reining also offers more successfully the establishment of free forward movement in the horse. The co-ordination of rein contact and use of the voice should create a better foundation for further training and an improved understanding of direction than would otherwise have been gained by lungeing. Peter prefers to use a saddle throughout this stage of breaking to avoid the need of changing from a roller just before backing. By shortening the leathers as much as possible the long reins can be passed through them, one on either side, and used more safely than they would be if they were lower.

Obviously all horses mature at quite different rates: where some are ready to start work at four years of age others are not sufficiently developed, either physically or mentally, until the age of perhaps five or six. So often, big horses, i.e. those over 16.2 h.h., may be six or seven before they are adult. Following the principle that no horse should be asked to work if there is a danger of him straining himself, it is very much up to the rider or trainer to assess when a young horse is capable of beginning schooling work.

All Peter's horses are hunted as youngsters because he believes it acts as a valuable foundation to the future education of a competition horse. Later on, if a horse is good enough for top-class jumping he is probably too valuable to risk injury in the hunting field. Hopefully, though, if the training and amount of pressure put on a horse throughout his work programme have been properly executed, he shouldn't be so jaded that he needs to go hunting to freshen him up. It should always be in the back of the rider's mind that the horse is having just the right amount of jumping so that he will not go over the top.

One of the rules of getting a horse fit is to allow plenty of time. Peter maintains that you have to be prepared to spend as long as a horse needs, not only in terms of minutes per day but also in the overall period between bringing him up and his first competition. It is vitally important not to bring a horse to fitness too quickly. This is detrimental to the length of time he will last, not just in any one season but for his whole competitive career. The more time that is spent bringing a horse into work, within reason, every single year of his life, is a sound investment in the horse's welfare in general and which will decide the number of years of soundness and performance that he can offer you. The significance of knowing each horse will enable you to keep him fresh and happy in his job. This is essential if you want his co-operation.

The amount of schooling a horse can take in any one

session will largely depend on his temperament and degree of cooperation. Peter tries to set a programme at the beginning of the season for each horse, bearing in mind that the older horses should need less schooling work before their first competition; nevertheless their preparation for fitness is still meticulous. Generally speaking eight to ten weeks is enough, so in preparing for their summer season which begins in April, the horses are 'brought up' at the beginning of February. For all of them the first two weeks are spent walking on the roads, beginning on one day with, say, thirty minutes on a long but not loose rein and gradually building up to one hour a day, by which time each horse should be walking into his bridle. The following two weeks of road work are used to bring jogging or slow trotting into the one-hour exercise. Half a mile of jogging at a stretch is interspersed with walking so that, gradually, the jogging is transformed into a correct trotting pace.

Peter is particularly keen on trotting, especially up and down hills because it produces the right type of fitness required of a show-jumper. He gauges the amount of fittening work in distance rather than time and would plan to be trotting for half a mile and walking for a quarter alternately for five, six or seven miles depending on the horse, by the middle of the second month (i.e. five to six weeks from the start). At about this stage gentle cantering begins and most horses are ready to start their ground work. Peter prefers that each horse does his road work before he is schooled each day to enable the horse to warm up whilst relaxing mentally. It is essential to 'play it by ear' and vary the location used for schooling because some horses work better away from the jumping paddock. It also pre-empts their anticipation as to when and where they might be asked to work. Somedays, as an alternative to his routine, a horse may be taken for a quiet hack away from the place he associates with schooling. This is a psychological tactic designed to prevent boredom setting in. From time to time, a day's exercise means a fun ride around the farm, jumping event-type fences. This teaches the horses to adapt to jumping at a cross-country pace as opposed to the collected form expected of a show-jumper.

Peter also has the benefit of a grass gallop at home to enable him to check his horses' wind and fitness but it must be remembered that horses are individuals and not every horse will benefit from a gallop.

Whatever the stage of training, each horse is walked for at least fifteen to twenty mminutes before being schooled. The jumping paddock on Peter's farm is far enough away from the stables to ensure that horses who go there directly from their boxes have had sufficient time to loosen up on the way. Depending entirely on the individual, an educated horse is schooled for fifteen to eighteen minutes. A rider must, of course, allow more time if he is not achieving the required results. One of the golden rules of schooling as far as Peter is concerned, is to have a plan of work for each horse *every* day and to not be satisfied until that target is reached. He believes that you should never be content with second-best either because a horse will soon learn that he can take advantage of you.

Other important points he bears in mind when schooling a young horse are: (1) Teach him one thing at a time – if you try to teach two things simultaneously the horse may become confused; and (2) Never ask too much too soon, or pose a question that the horse is insufficiently prepared, either mentally or physically, to answer. He considers the horse's education as rungs of a ladder, always starting at the bottom and satisfying himself that the pupil has fully understood the previous lesson before beginning the next. This way the horse can indicate his ability to learn and is not pushed beyond his capabilities at any time.

As the ground work advances so too will the horse's standard of fitness. It is therefore essential to carry out the right sort of exercises within the schooling programme to be sure of arriving at the competition with a supple and obedient horse. To this end Peter jumps each horse two or three times a week. In developing and toning up the correct muscles, various forms of gymnastics are used. Combinations of uprights and oxers, grids and 'pop-poles' (a pole placed on the ground a few feet in front of a fence), are wonderful exercises for any horse. Some horses need a lot of jumping preparation while others perform better in competition for hardly ever jumping at home.

The end of a lesson, having achieved a satisfactory result on which to build.

During the summer season Peter's horses have two rest periods, each lasting anything from a few days up to two weeks. The horse's competition schedule and how he is performing will guide the rider throughout the season and influence the decision as to when to rest him and for how long. If he is becoming bored or a bit jaded it will invariably mean that his winning ability is fading so a revision of his programme must be dealt with promptly.

Peter found that time and time again a mid-season rest of about eight to ten days followed by a small show a few days before a major event would be the ideal preparation for arriving at the big class with a horse who is mentally fresh and ready to give his best performance. The purpose of the visit to a small show would be merely to test the horse's fitness and readiness to compete rather than to go to win. Peter would then have a few days before the big class to adjust the training if necessary and be more assured of the horse's co-operation.

At the end of the summer season, which by tradition concludes with the Horse of the Year Show at Wembley in October, those horses who are to be rested begin to be 'let down'. Over a period of about two weeks their concentrate ration is adjusted to include more mashes, which cool down the horse's blood system. Hard food is cut down and more hay is fed. The time spent turned out is lengthened as the weather allows and any rugs are gradually removed. Once they are considered to be constitutionally roughed off they are turned away for the winter, i.e. October until February.

In Peter's opinion the qualities of a show-jumping rider should be a good temperament (not short-tempered); a willingness to learn; an ability to learn from mistakes; great application; open-mindedness; and the enthusiasm to work hard on a regular basis.

Peter feels that too many horses today, through inadequacies, compete before they are ready. Performance and the number of seasons of repetitive competitions that a horse will withstand will always depend on a combination of correct schooling and proper fitness. Obviously, then, the better prepared a horse is the better performance one can expect from him. This theory should be in the minds of all riders in order to keep the horse sweet and enjoying his work. Many of the top show-jumpers are able to stay at the top because they study the horses' requirements and can apply that understanding better than the average person. Your goal is to produce an attentive and supple horse who, over a period of two to three minutes, will offer you a jumping performance which displays the evidence of months of careful training to its fullest potential. There is no short cut to success and a properly trained and fit horse will last you longer than one who is only half trained and half as fit. Even the most carefully prepared horses do not escape injury or lameness forever but as long as you have done all that you can to minimise the effects of overstress, the quality and speed of recovery will be more efficient than for a horse who is fatigued and therefore has a lower threshold of resistance.

9 Eventing

Virginia Holgate

It would seem inevitable that someone born with so much natural talent and ability is bound to succeed at their chosen sport, given the necessary dedication and determination. Ginny is no exception to this having ridden since she was three years old, her family having always encouraged her in her riding ambitions. Although a lot of her early childhood was spent abroad in less horsey orientated environments she was not to be distracted from horses. When she did return to this country permanently and with the usual enthusiasm with which ponies somehow manage to infect teenage girls, she was soon discovered by Sally Strachan in the West Country. It was here that Ginny had her first riding lessons and by the age of sixteen, when Dubonnet arrived on the scene, her first attempt at eventing was made. This partnership, the first of many, was to carry her through the junior ranks into the international eventing world. Her continual competitive successes, both at home and overseas as a team member, have established her as one of our leading event riders proving that no matter what your background it is possible to compete on equal terms with other competitors who may have had the benefit of the Pony Club to establish themselves as riders.

Not only has she been getting horses fit for eventing for several years now, but also her record shows that from the high standard of fitness which her horses attain her methods are indeed an example to follow. This is undoubtedly because she is so skilled in the art of preparing horses for the ever-increasing demands of three-day eventing. The challenge of perfecting the three disciplines which comprise this sport is ever-present and when Ginny is mildly satisfied with one she finds that the other two invariably need more attention. Even after a

Virginia Holgate riding Welton Elan. Note the rider's position, balanced and ready to help the horse.

successful competition she will question herself as to whether the horse could have been fitter or whether she could have improved his performance. The standards in each discipline of eventing are being raised continually, making the sport highly competitive and dividing the men from the boys right from novice level. Only by analysing each horse's fitness programme after careful monitoring throughout all its stages can we hope to improve the quality of performance at the next outing. Ginny is a fine example, for no matter how brilliant you are at competing you can never afford to be complacent about the standard of fitness or level of success.

With the increase in popularity which this sport is enjoying at present it has been found necessary to help accommodate the number of competitors by introducing more events and encourage still more to be held. The result being that the spring and autumn seasons are now merging, effectively reducing the period of summer rest for the horses. This applies mostly to one-day events although candidates for the British three-day event team need an even more carefully planned schedule throughout a twelve-month period.

Ginny's eventers begin their preparation for the spring season soon after Christmas but she believes that some horses may even need to come into work before this. For example, a horse who has been rested since September would benefit from starting walking in mid-December if his first competition is to be at the beginning of March. The first two weeks for all the horses is spent walking, initially for half an hour, building up to one and a half hours. This is mainly carried out on the roads using hills as much as possible. After two or three weeks most of the horses are ready to begin some flat work on soft ground and after four weeks they can start to do proper hill work.

Once every three days each horse is lunged for about

forty minutes, which would include five minutes' cantering for the youngsters and about ten minutes for the
advanced horses. Working on the lunge at this stage
affords the opportunity for the horse to begin his collected work without the weight of the rider, thus toning up
muscles in preparation for the dressage schooling.

Usually at four to five weeks, the flat work becomes
part of the daily work routine (except for those in interval training). Around twenty to thirty minutes is
spent in the outdoor, all-weather surfaced arena, after
which the horse is taken out on road work for one to one
and a half hours. It is found, though, that some horses
work better if they have their road work before they are
schooled.

One day each week is spent in the arena doing grid
work, a form of gymnastics designed to make the horse
supple and athletic whilst teaching him to jump
correctly. Providing common sense is applied with
patient application the horse will develop confidence
which will carry him through more demanding exercises.
This is crucial for young horses, whose success depends
on sympathetic teaching and on never asking them too
much too soon.

The importance of a slow start to any horse's training
programme dictates just when to begin trotting and for
how long each day. Once the trotting has been built up
to suit the individual horse and represents at least
twenty-five per cent of the daily work routine, cantering
is introduced. Generally speaking this is sometime
during the second month. Exactly when will depend on
several things not least the level of the ultimate goal, be
it a three-day event, two-day intermediate or a series of
one-day events for a novice. Other equally important
factors are the time of year, how long the horse has been
rested and, above all, the type of horse. Usually the
horses are cantered twice a week before the start of the

season and once they are competing this is reduced to once a week at home. The advanced horses enjoy the luxury of a six-furlong all-weather gallop during the final month prior to a three-day event.

Ginny's strategy for cantering the advanced horses is based on interval training methods although she is keen to point out that her interpretation is a variation designed around each horse's particular requirements. The underlying principle is the same throughout: namely, a period of exertion followed by an interval of partial recovery before repeating the fast work. Over the course of a week Ginny will usually carry out the interval training on alternate days. After an initial warm-up trot which lasts for between five and fifteen minutes depending on the horse's requirements, canter sessions interspersed with periods of walking begin. At the start the routine may be as follows:

> 4 minutes canter
> 3 minutes walk
> 5 minutes canter
> 3 minutes walk
> 5 minutes canter

The exercise finishes with a walk to give the horse long enough for his respiration to return to normal while cooling off.

After six weeks, providing the horse has suffered no set-backs, the canter times will have increased and the recovery intervals decreased, so the timetable looks something like:

> 9 minutes canter
> 2 minutes walk
> 9 minutes canter
> 2 minutes walk
> 9 minutes canter

A welcome wash-down after a period of fast work on a hot day. Note the horse is still blowing even though his heart rate has stabilised. This was due to the extreme humidity.

During the first three weeks the cantering is done at a working pace; after that the last minute of the final canter each day is carried out at a slightly faster rate. In the final month before a three-day event the speed of the cantering is based on 570 metres per minute for the first two canters and 690 mpm (i.e. steeplechase – Phase B speed) for the last one. Care is taken to build up to the faster speed towards the end of the final training period before the event because working a horse too fast too soon is often the cause of injury.

As a guideline three months is allowed to prepare the eventer for his first competition when he is brought up from grass. If after ten weeks a horse appears to be fit enough for a minor competition, his standard and quality of fitness would be put to the test. Ginny finds that some horses reach and maintain optimum fitness if they are worked little and often rather than for long periods at a time. Care is always taken to protect the horses' legs by fitting boots whenever they are worked or turned out, but for cantering, tendon protectors are used as an additional safeguard.

To encourage a tough constitution which will help the horses to withstand the rigours of an endurance-type competitive life Ginny feels they should be turned out as much as the weather allows. A very careful eye must be kept on each horse though, especially as his fitness progresses, to ensure that he does not catch a chill.

Immediately after cantering the horses Ginny takes their respiration rates and temperatures as a means of monitoring their progress. It has been suggested earlier in this book (page 60) that TPR rates are an invaluable indicator for judging fitness and a guide for future training schedules. Allowances should be made for the effects which extreme weather conditions may have on some horses. Ginny also uses a heart-rate monitor (not on herself though!) during the fast work which gives her a constant reading of the horse's reaction. The monitor is attached under the girth on the heart area and connected, via a lead, to a unit on the rider's wrist or thigh. Thus he or she is enabled to follow more accurately the horse's fitness progress.

During the time that the horses are in training they are turned out each day after work for thirty to forty minutes, preferably without too much grass in the paddock. As a safeguard against legs swelling up, which so often occurs with stabled horses, each horse is led out for a few minutes in the afternoon to stimulate his circulation. In normal circumstances all the horses are worked for six days a week and given a complete rest on the seventh when they are turned out in the field. At the end of the season, after their final competition they are ridden for about two weeks as part of their 'letting down'. Concentrates are reduced and clothing gradually removed until they have adapted to staying out overnight.

The length of holiday each horse has is decided by his future plans. The summer vacation might only last for four to six weeks whereas the winter break is likely to start in October and end at Christmas time. By the end of the season the rider should know just how long it takes to get each horse fit and which methods suit him best. This is when the stable diary will show its value, providing of course that nothing has been omitted!

Like most successful yards, Ginny has a tremendous team behind her, led by her mother Heather and trainer Dorothy Willis. Working pupils are taken on a twelve-month basis and between them they look after up to ten stabled horses plus those animals who live out but who may be in work. Home for Ginny is only a short distance from the site of Britain's most prestigious three-day event: Badminton, which would seem appropriate. Although the Holgates have only ten acres on which to house their competition horses, careful management of the land ensures that the grassland is utilised efficiently. To get the best out of it, lime is spread once a year and a neighbour's cattle serve to keep the grass short. Because of the limited grazing, any horses on holiday are farmed out to local farmers. It is a very strict policy, despite being time-consuming, to collect all droppings off the land each and every day as a precaution against worm infestation.

Feeding practices in the Holgate yard are kept as traditional as possible with priority given to feeding the very best quality feedstuffs available. Any change in a batch of feed is avoided once the horses are in work, and with the help of local feed merchants supplying large quantities this is usually possible. Any alterations in diet are made over four to five days to allow the horse to benefit without disrupting his digestive system. Where additives are fed, natural substances are chosen in preference to manufacturers' preparations as the latter may contain several ingredients including some which may not be needed. Limestone flour is fed to all horses at all stages of fitness and an eggspoonful of cod liver oil would be the most a horse is given. Cubed grassmeal is fed after it has been soaked for twelve hours and, apart from seaweed and common salt, the rest of the diet comprises conventional food. Heather also has a mix and a cube prepared by her feed merchants according to her specifications. The Holgates' principles of feeding are basically to ensure that the horses do not go for long periods without food but not to overface them. This involves giving small portions of hay between feeds which helps to amuse them and prevent boredom. The importance of adhering to the horse's natural habits, one of which is feeding little and often, has already been pointed out in Chapter 2. The following table details an average diet for an event horse in the last six weeks prior to his first event of the season.

7 a.m.	1 p.m.	5 p.m.	9 p.m.
2lbs oats	2lbs oats	2lbs oats	2lbs oats
2lbs sugar-beet	2lbs sugar-beet	2lbs sugar-beet	2lbs sugar-beet
2lbs grassmeal	2lbs grassmeal	2lbs grassmeal	2lbs grassmeal
double handful chaff	double handful chaff	double handful chaff	double handful chaff
1 lb mix		2 oz salt	
		eggspoonful cod liver oil	
		handful seaweed	
		handful limestone flour	

It must be stressed that this is *only a guideline* based on an opinion and any quantities must be adjusted according to each animal's specific requirements.

In the normal course of events a day's routine in the Holgate yard will begin at 6.30 a.m. when the horses are fed their first ration of either hay or haylage. All the conventional hay is soaked for twenty-four hours before feeding to safeguard against any possibility of damaging the horse's respiratory system through hay dust. Fifteen minutes later the horses are fed and once they have finished they are mucked out. Water buckets are then cleaned and refilled and the boxes set fair before the staff go to breakfast. The morning is spent working the horses, some of whom will be strapped once they have been out in the paddock. They then are given their second portion of hay/haylage before being fed at one o'clock. A further portion of hay/haylage is then given in the middle of the afternoon. Once all the horses are exercised and have been out in the paddock, the grooming complete, the rest of the afternoon is taken up with the endless chores which surround a competition yard. The horses' tea-time is normally 5 p.m. after which they are fed more hay/haylage. Those horses who receive a fourth feed will be given it after the final evening stables are carried out at 9 p.m.

In such a busy yard, with horses coming and going in all directions, an efficient and organised team of staff is essential. There are always numerous maintenance jobs to be done but the priority is the horses' welfare, around which everything revolves.

The routine during a competition will obviously depend on how much travelling is involved, but naturally the feeding is adjusted accordingly, allowing plenty of time for the horse to digest his food before exercise. If there is time between the dressage and show-jumping phase of a one-day event the horse is given a small feed. He is not allowed water for the last three hours before he is scheduled to go cross country, but if he is to run late in the day he would be permitted a small portion of haylage early. In the case of a three-day event his water is removed four hours prior to him running, and his hay ration is halved the night before with any left-overs removed by 6 a.m. on the morning of cross-country day. The only alteration to the concentrates ration is that sugar-beet is left out of the morning feed on cross-country day.

Once the horse has stopped blowing after his cross-country effort, he is offered a quarter of a bucket of luke-warm water at half-hourly intervals until he is drinking in moderation, at which time he is allowed to have water *ad lib*. At all times, both at home and away, if the weather is cold and damp, the chill is taken off the water for horses who have just worked because Ginny believes it helps them to recover. It must be stressed that any routine, whether it be in the yard or at a competition, is applied only to horses who show absolutely no signs of distress or abnormality. For example a horse who appears distressed for an unusually long time after his cross-country round should not be allowed to drink too much water too soon. However confident you are of the quality of your horse's fitness you should watch his behaviour extra carefully after a period of prolonged exertion. Failure to act when a horse is overstressed and possibly in need of veterinary attention could damage his health not only in the short term but also more permanently.

With event horses, perhaps more so than in other disciplines, there are additional factors peculiar to their endurance-type fitness preparation which must be taken into account. To ignore any climatic or environmental changes taking place is to run the risk of harming the horse both short and long term because he may be subjected to additional stress without due compensation.

The problems caused by competing in extreme heat and humidity are becoming more apparent now, even in Britain's temperate climate. For a horse selected to compete abroad in a hot climate the problem is more serious if he has not had a chance to acclimatise.

An illustration of this situation arose during Ginny's preparation of Night Cap for the European Championships in 1983. Much of his fast work was carried out in the height of an uncharacteristically hot summer, which at times was also very humid. It was clear that this horse took twice as long to recover from the same amount of work in conditions of extreme humidity. Even when his heart rate had stabilised, his respiration took much longer to settle down. This type of weather conditions was prevalent in Switzerland during those championships but to a greater extent. To counteract their effect on the horse, Ginny held a bag of ice over his neck during Phase C (second roads and tracks). Immediately after the cross country iced water was again used and it was found that once the horse had recovered from his exertions, he suffered no apparent ill-effects as a result of the weather.

Like many riders Ginny has found that if her horses sweat profusely in hot weather they benefit enormously from being washed down liberally with cold water and sweat-scraped thoroughly. This clears the skin pores most efficiently of their fluid secretion and subsequently cools the blood system more quickly.

From her experience gained by training and competing in hot and humid conditions Ginny feels that in future she will make a point of working the horses at home during the hottest time of the day to help them acclimatise. Also she recommends that horses are clipped after the dressage phase of a three-day event if the same hot conditions prevail. Whilst we are constantly learning how best to cope with new situations found in competitions it is always hoped that any discoveries are made available to all competitors.

1984 saw another Olympic Games in Los Angeles but unlike the last Games held there competitors were able to benefit from the scientific information gained over recent years and were more prepared to counteract the severe stress conditions, caused mainly by the climate, to which the horses were subjected. Oxygen was constantly available for the horses in case the Los Angeles smog combined with the high temperatures and humidity distressed them unduly. Generally, though, if the horses were suitably fit for the competition they coped with the conditions very well and recovered from the fast work quite satisfactorily.

Another condition to which endurance horses are susceptible is dehydration. The climate will again make a difference to the degree of effect and just how it is dealt with depends on when it occurs during the course of a competition. Traditionally eventers are never allowed water for three to four hours before the speed and endurance phase of an event. On the other hand long-distance riding horses are penalised if they are found to be suffering from dehydration before and after a competition. It poses the question: why not allow the eventer a small drink of water to sip during the ten-minute interval (i.e. after the second roads and tracks), and why deprive him for so long beforehand? Surely the longer he is without, the thirstier he becomes even without body fluid loss (though it is accepted that he does not need a full stomach of food or water before a lot of exercise). We must not forget, however, that his requirements will change as his fitness progresses in terms of appetite both for food and water. Electrolytes (minerals and salts) are being used more widely by eventing people, usually after the speed and endurance phase. Glucose has long been a more traditional substance offered to eventers during the ten-minute interval before the cross-country phase of a three-day event, usually by sponging the mouth. It is a source of energy but as with electrolytes is it still debatable whether the horse actually suffers from their absence as a result of exertion particularly if he is on a well-balanced diet and receiving all the vitamins and minerals he normally requires.

Most of our top competitors find it is beneficial to their own fitness if they have some other exercise besides riding and Ginny is no exception. In preparing for a season of strenuous competitions she plays squash and tennis but she feels that skipping every day is particularly useful for improving condition. Fitness, both in limbs and wind, is all-important to the quality of your riding. It is therefore up to you to prepare yourself in order to do justice to the horse by riding him to your fullest potential.

10 Showing

Robert Oliver

Robert's vast experience of showing began at the Eckleys' famous Cusop stud when he was afforded the wonderful opportunity of showing high-class ponies – the ideal start for any aspiring show rider. After ponies Robert moved on to riding hunters and hacks which helped him to develop his natural, relaxed style of riding which encourages his show horses to present themselves so well in the ring.

Robert feels that without some background in equestrianism, be it in show-jumping, eventing or showing, it can be very difficult for anyone to become established as a showman in the ring. This is not necessarily because your face doesn't fit but rather that you need a certain amount of natural aptitude and an outgoing personality in order to show an animal successfully. Each horse requires individual and specialist attention in order to exhibit its paces to their fullest potential before a particular judge or judges. In Robert's opinion the very art of showing is to become sufficiently relaxed that the horse carries you, rather than you having to work on him the whole time.

Apart from the obvious requirements of good conformation, the show horse must have a placid and obedient temperament if he is to cope with the extra-ordinary atmosphere of the horse show. Combined with these attributes the show animal must exude tremendous presence and give the rider a sense of power while behaving obediently for each judge whatever his way of riding.

Lord Sorcerer, a small hunter, was the first Wembley champion that Robert rode at the Horse of the Year Show in the early 1970s. Clearly making his mark on the showing world with experience founded in the hunting field and in the Pony Club, Robert felt he should establish his own business. His subsequent successes, born of his exceptional qualities as a horseman, qualify him as an authority on the fitness and conditioning of the show horse for every type of class.

Together with his wife Gillian (née Blakeway), Robert runs a yard of twenty-five boxes from his home in north Gloucestershire.

All year round these stables are full of top-quality animals ranging from show horses to potential eventers and steeplechasers at various stages of their education. Every type of show horse and pony is prepared here from in-hand youngstock to children's ponies, hacks, cobs, working hunters and hunters for the ladies and weight classes. Part of their early training may include some hunting and travelling to a few local shows as an introduction to public life before they concentrate on competing themselves.

Robert is a great advocate of the use of long-reining which he believes is a wonderful method of educating the young horse. He claims his horses wear out a set of shoes during the time they are 'driven' around the country lanes so that when they are ready to be backed and ridden away they are very familiar with all the normal sights and sounds they will encounter from day to day. No doubt this method of early training is the

Robert Oliver and Celtic Gold, immaculately turned out.
(Bob Langrish)

foundation on which Robert's horses' confidence and relaxed style of performing is built. Added to this is Robert's natural talent for bringing out the best in each horse by patient and individual attention to every aspect of the horse's welfare and preparation.

Whilst money can buy the horse for the job, it cannot provide any whirlwind successes without someone doing a great deal of work. Many of the more wealthy owners of show horses are fortunate in being able to call upon the services and talent of recognised producers to prepare their horses for the ring. For the majority, however, we have to learn the hard way before success is achieved and this, as in all sports, can take months and years.

Robert's team of family and staff operate a highly efficient yard which keeps them busy all the year round, not only with the horses' work but also with the management aspects of running a business. This involves considerable paperwork for show entries, the registration of horses, and informing owners of their horses' movements. In addition there are always horses to view, which can involve a great deal of travelling. His yard, although buzzing with activity throughout the day, is always kept tidy and well maintained. The stables include a barn system with four boxes made of brick with a high roof offering good ventilation. This ensures that the horses are warm in the winter and cool in the summer. The main doorway to the barn in the central passageway is never closed, allowing the horses to look out across the yard and not become bored. On the other side of the yard are six boxes measuring 12ft × 12ft, of breeze block construction. These, because they face south, tend to get too hot for the horses in the summer; in severe winter, however, the horses in these boxes could become too cold without their top doors closed. Behind these boxes are a further eight stables and facing west are four more larger boxes of 16ft × 14ft which house the middle to heavyweight hunters, who in Robert's opinion do better for being in a bigger box. Any horse who comes to the Olivers' yard is taught strict stable manners and required to stand whilst being tended to for as long as necessary, which is of course a priority in the show ring. It would be an exception to find any horse in this yard lay back his ears or threaten you in any way, which reflects the respect the horses have for their attendants.

Robert is fortunate in having a covered school of 60ft × 60ft which he uses mainly for schooling the mature, well-balanced horses. He feels that the youngsters who are 'green' and unbalanced are not able to cope with working in a confined space so a lot of their schooling is done whilst out hacking round the country lanes. Much of the Olivers' success is attributed to the variety of work which all the horses are given, and to the fact that there is no hard and fast rule for any one of them. During their exercising they are made to negotiate all manner of natural hazards. It is felt that teaching them simple exercises such as opening and closing gates quietly and patiently, is of fundamental importance to their preparation for the show ring and serves to develop confidence on which performance is built.

The horse's obedience is crucial as far as Robert is concerned, no matter in what situation the horse is placed. The rider must aim at presenting smooth transitions without resistance. Simple basic tack is used at home such as the snaffle bridle and drop nose-band, and in the event of a horse needing a martingale, a standing rather than a running one is used because Robert prefers to have the pressure on the horse's nose rather than on the bars of the mouth. Simple exercises comprise the show horse's daily schooling work and it must be remembered that the show horse will always be expected to perform on the right rein. In an effort to encourage suppleness and obedience they are taught simple changes of rein, fluent transitions in fairly small circles and to rein back.

The show horse must have developed a hard condition by the time the first shows start at the beginning of May if he is to withstand the rigours of the season which ends in October at the Horse of the Year Show. Not only will he need a firm and round state of fitness for the actual competitions but the travelling also places demands on the horse and, if not prepared, he will suffer eventually from this repetitive stress. Almost anyone can prepare *a* horse for one particular competition but the secret of success lies in the ability to maintain the quality of condition in different horses throughout the season. Nor can the horse's mental state be overlooked, because once he becomes bored and uninterested his natural presence will not be there to catch the judge's eye.

The staff begin their daily routine at 7.30 a.m. with feeding and mucking out. After breakfast the exercising begins. When the hacking is done the second and third groups of horses are schooled. In the normal daily routine all the horses are worked in the morning and those who do not have to go out again are groomed. Shampooing is done regularly in this yard after the horses have worked but exceptional care is taken to dry off the horses thoroughly either by leading them out or jogging them on the lunge – and in twenty years Robert has never had one horse catch a chill. He makes a point of turning out all the horses for an hour or two on fine days once the season begins. He believes they need the chance to relax in natural surroundings to help them endure a competitive life without taking any more out of themselves than is necessary. If any of the horses become tense and show signs of going over the top they would then be turned out daily and not worked for, say, a week or so to encourage them to unwind. Robert says he has had some horses who have not been ridden at all between one show and the day before the next but instead have been turned out to grass. No doubt these are exceptions and there would have to be no danger of the horse losing too much condition from the rest. Likewise, those horses who are likely to become jarred up on hard ground in mid-summer would be given a half-term holiday of between two and four weeks depending on their age and temperament.

Horses in an average state, that is neither too fat nor too thin, are brought up on March 1st with the intention of beginning their show season in the first week of May. Starting with half an hour's walking they will have built up by the end of the third week to one hour a day. Trotting and schooling begins at four weeks and by the end of six weeks the daily work schedule for most horses totals one and a half hours. This involves either working in the arena, lungeing or long-reining depending on their stage of training. If the fields are too muddy the horses are worked either in the school at home or taken to a nearby indoor arena. Although schooling work is obviously a necessary part of the show horse's exercise, care must be taken not to overdo it because it can often be the cause of a horse's wind becoming stuffy. After the end of March the horses are made to do hill work and some half-speed cantering with the purpose of keeping their air passages clear. A judge will soon spot a horse who is short of a canter and criticise an exhibitor for showing an animal with congested respiration.

Robert feeds his horses on conventional foods and his methods are based on traditional ideas. He does not use any modern supplements or additives apart from cod liver oil. So many show people today tend to spend a fortune on stoking up their horses with expensive concoctions which, judging by Robert's successful results, are not always necessary. Providing the feed you use is of the best available quality, show horses like any others can clearly be conditioned on a basic diet of oats, bran, sugar-beet, chaff, and horse and pony cubes. An average diet for the light- to middleweight hunter in show condition would be: 3lbs oats; 2lbs bran; 1lb sugar-beet; 1lb chaff as one feed, three times a day, i.e. 7.30 a.m., 12.30 p.m., and 5.30 p.m. In some cases, particularly with the hacks, the oats may be substituted for horse and pony cubes. Only occasionally does Robert find it necessary to give a fourth feed—when a horse has lost some condition perhaps from travelling. In this case he would be fed after all the horses are checked at 9.30 p.m. Twice a week all horses are given a bran mash with Epsom salts. No one could deny that Robert's horses always look in superb condition throughout the season, proof that these simple feeding habits work for any type of show horse.

The clipping and rugging of show horses are a very important part of their stable management. When they first come into work a jute rug will usually be enough before they are clipped but in order to encourage them to shed their winter coats early they will need two or three blankets underneath the jute rug. Robert generally clips the horses right out, i.e. hunter clip, depending on their breed, because the more commonly bred horse tends to hold his coat more than, say, a Thoroughbred would.

The way in which a horse is turned out for the show ring will have a great deal of influence on the judge's overall assessment of the animal. Good conformation and action form only part of the presentation and no judge will tolerate an untidy exhibit. It is therefore an essential part of stable management from the day the horse comes into work to see that mane and tail pulling, trimming and bandaging are given due consideration. There can be no short cuts and attention to detail here will be noticed equally as much as the rest of the horse. It will be seen with successful competitors that to achieve reward for the months of careful preparation, no stone can be left unturned. This should be remembered throughout every aspect of the show horse's management, from tack cleaning to shoeing, and turn-out to condition. Saddlery must be correct in every way and as clean and highly polished as it can be. Selection of the show animal is only the beginning and most competitors use methods which are private to them; these are their tricks of the trade and they would be loath to give them away. Experience will, however, teach you to pick up these idiosyncrasies and develop them to your advantage because it is such details which so often make the difference between success and disappointment in the ring.

In selecting an animal for the show ring you have to have a comprehensive understanding of conformation, action and temperament in order to be able to identify each horse's potential. It won't always be possible to view the horse in a show condition: sometimes, especially when buying a youngster who is perhaps unbroken, the horse will be in a rough state, possibly covered in mud. Poor condition can easily disguise a horse's attributes and the keen eye of a horseman will be able to interpret whether or not the horse will be capable of the kind of performance required of the show horse. Each type of show class demands different qualitites with which you need to be completely familiar. Often you can recognise those horses who have been produced by one of the top exhibitors, for they invariably look for the same type of animal, i.e. with a sloping shoulder, straight hind leg, deep girth and nicely set on head and neck. Robert explains that horses with these basic qualities always seem to do well and are consequently easier to maintain in show condition for the whole season.

The horses' feeding routine during the day of a competition is not changed any more than is necessary to accommodate the classes. Unlike other competition horses, they are allowed hay and water *ad lib* and are given a feed before their return journey home. Robert likes them to have some grass whenever possible, even if it means picking some to add to their hay-net.

At the end of the season if a horse is to go jumping in preparation for working hunter classes or eventing, he might be lightly hunted before Christmas. For the rest of the horses it marks the start of their winter holiday. The roughing-off process is carried out over a period of three to four weeks, during which time rugs would be removed in the day. Robert makes a point of letting the horses down gradually because there is always a danger of their losing condition which would be difficult to replace before the onset of winter. Once he is happy that they are adequately hardened off and if the weather is suitable, the half-bred horses and the ponies are turned out. Other less hardy types are brought in at night. It must be remembered that the job of conditioning horses for any discipline will be less difficult if they have been done well during the winter months.

The whole process of fittening a show horse is no less an art than preparing an endurance horse who requires an athletic type of fitness. Only the eye of the master will be able to judge where and how each horse needs to lose or gain weight. When a horse first comes into work he must be carefully assessed to decide on his diet and programme of work. The latter, particularly in the initial stages of a fitness timetable, will need to be carried out gradually, especially with any horses not carrying much excess fat. If the early work is not stepped up gently this type of horse can easily develop muscularly while losing that large, round condition required of a show horse. On the other hand some horses who come in from their holiday in an overweight condition will need quite a different diet and programme in order to lose unwanted fat whilst retaining enough for the type of conditioning that is needed. A certain amount of fat is necessary for the show horse but too much can be extremely harmful, leading to heart disease and unsoundness both in wind and limbs. Care must be taken to ensure that you are not being cruel by overfeeding when mistakenly your kindness can be doing more harm than good. The second consideration when planning any horse's diet is the actual waste in terms of the food that the horse cannot utilise efficiently – and none of us can afford to throw money on the muck heap. It must be stressed that each

A six-year-old middleweight just before his first show of the season.

horse is different in his reaction to any training and must be regarded as such. There can be no hard and fast rules for the speed of progressing with each work pattern and anyone who tries to generalise with horses will soon find that they cannot achieve the quality of fitness, whatever the chosen discipline. Show horses, perhaps more than any others, do get criticised for being overweight and whilst we can follow an example such as Robert's for the feeding and work of an average horse, it must be remembered that this is *only a guideline*. The condition in which your horse arrives at a show must be left to your judgment, and common sense should guide you as to which methods you should use for any one horse. Also, you should always be prepared to change a policy if it proves unsuitable for a particular horse.

The actual competition day can often prove to be a long drawn-out affair with a great deal of waiting for a class to begin, and, depending on the size of the class, a lengthy wait before you perform your individual show. Hopefully the weather will be kind and make the day enjoyable, regardless of your achievements in the ring. A rain-soaked show with miserable horses and bedraggled riders usually needs some compensation in the form of rosettes to carry your spirits through. Patience is one of the first requirements of a show exhibitor because the delays are beyond anyone's control and once one class runs behind schedule the whole programme is inevitably disrupted. You have to be prepared for hold-ups and hitches with showing and if you find that after qualifying for the championship early in the morning you have to wait until late afternoon for the final parade, you must learn to be philosophical and make the best of your day out. Usually you will need help to strip the horse down in the ring and if you are not fortunate enough to have a groom, a friend or relative should be found because it is not easy for the rider to do everything on his own. If you are not paying someone for their help it would be courteous to show your appreciation in some way – after all, they are only doing it for your benefit. Showing, like all other sports, attracts a particular type of person and you will soon find that you can make many friends and enjoy the social aspect of the sport as well as the competition.

11 Polo

Claire Tomlinson

Claire's early introduction to polo was due to her father owning and running his own polo club. As a child she soon learnt to use a polo stick but there were not the opportunities for children in the Pony Club that there are now. When she went to Oxford University her competitive instincts were encouraged and the quality of her horsemanship and natural aptitude for the sport were soon spotted and put to good use in the university polo team. A more serious approach to the sport was adopted about fifteen years ago when she married and subsequently developed her interests in the breeding, training and playing of polo ponies from her home in Gloucestershire. For several years now Claire has ranked amongst the finest polo players in the world, as good as any man and indeed better than many. Her utter devotion to the art of the game is portrayed by her sensitive handling of the ponies. To her they are far more than just a vehicle on which to travel from one end of the pitch to the other. Through sympathetic riding she forms a partnership with her pony in a demonstration of stylish co-ordination which enables them to play the game in harmony and with economy of effort. Claire's team loyalties lie with the high-goal team called Los

Locos with whom she plays alongside her husband Simon. Happily for the polo world her skills are being passed down to her children.

Sadly there is no doubt that polo as a sport has been given a bad image by a few people who mistakenly think that it can be bad for your riding. The reverse is the case, for, as Claire explains, a high standard of equitation and good eye are prerequisites for the polo player and it is a gross error for an aspiring rider to consider playing polo before he has achieved a competent level of horsemanship. As a galloping sport with so much stopping and turning it requires a confident rider who allows his pony to go forward freely at speed. At such a fast pace an insecure rider would become unbalanced and, through grabbing the reins for support, would consequently unbalance the pony. An independent seat born of an accomplished horseman, co-ordination and a quick eye together with a sympathetic handling of the pony, combine the essential ingredients of the polo player.

The game involves endless changes of direction so the pony's agility is crucial. He must be taught to go slightly behind the bit and completely off his forehand. A well-balanced pony in self-carriage will be able to perform movements at speed without relying on the bit. It is for this reason that artificial aids such as standing martingales or running reins are fitted to give the pony's head a ceiling so helping him to balance when applying the brakes. It is common practice to over-bit a polo pony by, say, using a double bridle or a gag to encourage him to come behind the bit. A simpler bit such as a snaffle might be inclined to damage the pony's mouth because polo ponies do tend to get hold of the bit and lean more easily. The pony is taught to neck-rein with a light contact on the mouth, the rider's weight distribution playing a large part in manoeuvring the animal. A gag or pelham distributes pressure to the poll area with a

Claire Tomlinson (right) riding off Prince Charles.
(Bob Langrish)

minimal effect on the corners and bars of the mouth. It does not necessarily follow that because the pony is wearing a lot of tack, his rider is incompetent and relies on gadgets to help his performance but rather the choice of tack is made to help the pony to manoeuvre efficiently with economy of effort.

To be able to keep up with the pace of the game a player must be fit in himself otherwise he would be out of breath before the end of the first chukka. If your riding pursuits only take place during the summer months it is an investment to prepare yourself physically during the winter. It is most unwise to expect the horse to get you fit when the season begins for you run the risk of straining muscles. Even if you ride throughout the year as Claire does, with hunting and breaking-in youngstock, some other form of exercise is recommended to get muscles sufficiently toned and breathing improved. Claire does some jogging and plays squash in preparation for the polo season. None of us then can afford to be complacent about our condition because if we are not in good shape it's not fair on the pony let alone your fellow team members.

Although Claire breeds many of her ponies she still buys in animals, sometimes from the Argentine. This Argentinian breed has long since established itself as a stamp of polo pony most suited to the game by virtue of size, type and temperament. The nature of the sport suggests that the pony needs to be tough, athletic and fast, with a handy turn of foot. Whilst performance is the overall priority, the pony must have reasonable conformation to withstand the demands of the game. Claire is prepared to overlook minor defects in conformation such as sickle hocks which predispose to curbs, because with all the sudden braking they have to do it is an advantage for them to have a natural tendency to bring their hocks under their body. The ideal height of the polo pony is 15 h.h., but anything between 14.3 h.h. and 16 h.h. is suitable, bearing in mind that a 15 h.h. Argentine pony would often be tougher and more capable of carrying a heavier person than a 15.2 h.h. Thoroughbred. Claire prefers mares on the whole, although her procedure for choosing a pony is based firstly on how the animal rides, secondly on how it plays and thirdly on its conformation. Using this method she can decide within a very short time whether an animal will be capable of the high standard of performance which is required of him in high-goal polo. Although the polo player is not looking for a show animal, care should be taken not to disregard defects in conformation which may manifest themselves as weaknesses once the pony is put under stress.

The way in which a pony responds at the start of his career, and indeed each season, will determine the quality and duration of his competitive life. Claire's ponies are ready to be introduced to the rudiments of the game at four years of age. When they are five they begin to play minor competitions so that by the time they reach their sixth year they should be ready for a full season of matches. The emphasis is always on keeping the ponies relaxed so they do not waste nervous energy by hotting up both before or during a game. Generally a pony would play one or two chukkas, each lasting seven minutes. Claire believes that the secret of keeping a pony fit throughout the season is *not* to play him more than one chukka per match at the beginning. The aim is to maintain optimum performance for as long as possible with each pony. Pushing him beyond his physical capabilities during work will only reduce his working life through overstress and render him more susceptible to injury. A tired pony may indicate fatigue by leaning on his bit towards the end of a chukka, but this is usually with a bad rider who does not recognise when to ease off. Hopefully, such a rider is in the minority. The ponies' resistance to injuries is invariably lower towards the end of the season when it will be seen that cuts and wounds take much longer to heal. With any form of riding, and especially in competitions, if you want a horse to respond willingly then you must not place him in a situation that he is unprepared to handle, physically and/or mentally.

Claire has a comparatively large yard which can accommodate up to thirty horses, all of whom may be in work at the same time. To care for so many horses in work requires about ten grooms. As well as the polo ponies getting fit there are a number of youngsters at different stages of their education. The training programme for the ponies preparing for a season begins in early March with the first few days being spent in the enclosed arena. They are ridden for ten to twenty minutes to get them used to being in work again and to encourage them to work off any excess energy caused by mischief. As well as walking and trotting they might also be cantered briefly; by first settling them in a confined space they are subsequently safer to take out on the roads. With so many horses to exercise it is not practical to ride each horse individually every day so they are taught to be led from one another. This way three horses can be exercised by one groom. Providing this is done correctly within a timetable it saves the horses' backs from too much pressure when they are unfit. The first week of road work comprises up to thirty minutes daily of brisk walking. A slow trot is introduced at the end of the first week over about two minutes. During the next three weeks the trotting is increased to ten-minute intervals, while at the same time decreasing the walking periods to five minutes. Total time spent on road work would now be one and a half hours. During this time the pony gradually begins schooling exercises in the arena to develop his athletic ability. These consist of suppling movements such as cavaletti work two or three times a week. Continuous road work at this stage would only serve to make him as fit as a hunter going in a straight line and not produce the gymnastic suppleness required.

Once cantering begins as part of their fitness programme, the daily training routine is split into two sessions. This is generally about three weeks before the first match. The morning work-out involves about one hour of road work and in the afternoon they are cantered or jogged for up to twenty minutes. Once they are fit and playing, which is usually two months from the start of their fitness programme, some ponies will have one hour's exercise in the morning and the same in the afternoon. They are galloped at half speed just to give them a pipe-opener and check that their wind is all right. Fast work on the day of a match, i.e. in the warm-up period, is not recommended as it tends to hot-up most ponies. It is most important to try and keep the ponies as relaxed as possible, not least just before the start of a game.

Claire believes that the most reliable way of judging the fitness of a pony is by playing him. How near he is to his carefully planned goal will be clearly demonstrated by his level of performance. One can then adjust his training accordingly, if indeed it is necessary.

The polo season begins at the end of April and ends in September. During that time a pony could be scheduled to play, on average, two matches per week plus possibly one practice session. Low-goal matches consist of four chukkas while high-goal games are made up of six. Once a pony is fit enough to be playing two chukkas he could be galloping for up to fourteen minutes plus a spell in the warm-up period. Assuming he is to retain this schedule for four months, he will obviously need a most carefully organised training routine from the day he first comes into work. Nor can it be forgotten that the aim is to try and keep him relaxed, which may require considerable patience from the rider as the pony becomes fitter. Anticipation of his reactions will, with sympathetic handling, minimise the effect of the stress which a competitive life will place on him and help him to enjoy the game as much as you do.

The day after a match, if the weather permits, the ponies are turned out for two or three hours. Alternatively they might be led out from another pony for just as long as it takes to relieve any stiffness by walking.

Roughing off can take from one to two weeks depending on how long the pony has been in work and, of course, the weather. During this time they are left out a bit longer each day and rugs are removed gradually, starting in the daytime and progressing until the pony can manage comfortably without them. The diet is simultaneously adjusted during this period by increasing the hay and decreasing the concentrates. Although Claire prefers to feed seed hay to the horses that are in work, she finds that once they are roughed off and when they run short of grass they do very well on good-quality silage which has been properly preserved, providing they have all the concentrates they need when the weather is hard. Ground barley and soya-bean meal replace the oats when the ponies are turned out, but whatever they receive, Claire is convinced that the animals' condition during the season depends a great deal on how well they are fed during the winter.

With so many horses in work it is virtually impossible to lay down a stringent feed list noting every change that may have been made throughout a season. As a guide though, their concentrate ration is gradually built up to around nine pounds of oats and seven pounds of race-horse nuts. Where horse and pony nuts replace race-horse nuts for some ponies, the maximum amount would be ten pounds of nuts to three to four pounds of oats. These quantities are for fit ponies who have started playing. Bran and salt are included in all the ponies' feeds and linseed is fed once a week. Most ponies are fed twice a day but a poor feeder would have his ration divided into three feeds.

Shoeing a polo pony is basically the same as for most competition horses, starting off with a heavier shoe when they begin their road work and fitting a lighter shoe once the fast work is introduced. The feet are trimmed slightly more than, say, for a hunter because the shoe must fit as tight to the toe as possible without making the foot 'boxy' in any way. A soft-centred stud is allowed to be fitted for playing; usually one is used in each hind shoe although two are permitted by the sport's ruling body.

Because of the nature of the sport it is essential that the ponies' legs are protected as much as possible during work, either with boots or with bandages. There is a higher risk of tendon injury and over-reaches in this sport than in most other disciplines, and this can mean weeks or months off work. Muscle injuries too are common and any treatment which reduces the recovery time has to be welcomed. Unlike eventers or show-jumpers, polo ponies have a relatively short season so an interruption as a result of injury, especially half way through the season, can effectively write a pony off for the rest of the year.

The role of Phenylbutazone is a controversial subject but where its use is permitted it has a part to play provided it is not abused. Claire is not in favour of its use as a means of disguising symptoms, and therefore pain, but agrees that its anti-inflammatory properties can be used successfully for curing acute soft tissue injuries such as a muscle strain. It is essential, though, that whatever the injury the animal must stop work immediately when unsoundness is noticed. Diagnosis and treatment should be made as early as possible and the pony rested from work until recovery is completely achieved. Working a horse before he is fully recovered is almost certain to aggravate any damaged tissue resulting in perhaps a more prolonged period of treatment and rest. Recurrence of an injury is evidence that it may not have been treated properly in the first place and did not heal as it should.

In conclusion then, the polo pony is rather like a sprinter who must perform at a high speed for short periods and will consequently tire quickly. Whilst his period of exertion may only last seven minutes it is up to us to ensure that through correct training he can achieve optimum performance with a minimum of stress. With this in mind he should be allowed complete rest and recovery in between work to keep him fresh in mind and body in the hope that he will enjoy the match as a game rather than as a job.

12 Driving

Cynthia Haydon

Cynthia Haydon needs little introduction, for her reputation as an expert with driving horses speaks for itself. Anyone with even a passing interest in the horse world will be familiar with her life-long achievements in this discipline. She inherited her enthusiasm and devotion to the sport from her father and grandfather and as a child showed ponies very successfully. Since then her extraordinary talent and natural aptitude have kept her in the forefront of the British and international driving scene, producing horses of all types from Hackneys to marathon teams. In true sportsmanlike tradition her quiet modesty belies her wealth of knowledge and this, together with her in-born talent, makes her a complete horsewoman.

Showing animals of any sort requires a professional and perfectionist approach if they are to be produced in an ideal condition and with nothing less than first-class turn-out. It is one thing to achieve this in one season but to maintain the high standard required, and at top level, year after year demands extra proficiency. Driving is, of course, a fairly expensive sport compared to riding because of the additional equipment that has to be bought and then maintained in show condition. It therefore calls for a team effort and hours of hard work but the pride and satisfaction of producing horse, harness and carriage in a polished show condition makes it all very worthwhile. It is easy to sympathise with competitors who, after patient preparation for a class, are subjected to a shower of rain, leaving them to exhibit their turn-out in the mud. But then it doesn't rain at every show, does it?

There are many types of classes for the driving enthusiast and apart from marathon events which demand an endurance-type fitness, most require a show condition in the horse that has to be maintained throughout the season. It is therefore a continual challenge to go through a season without the horse losing condition either from work or as a result of the necessary travelling, whilst retaining the essential presence and keenness which are the hallmarks of a successful competitor. An over-stressed horse who shows signs of boredom and tiredness is no competitor for the show ring and should be rested until such time as he has recovered both physically and mentally.

Cynthia has always been in the fortunate position of having a fairly large yard with a full complement of staff, both men and girls, to manage between twenty and thirty horses. She also breeds most of the horses that she shows so the yard is made up of both breeding stock and competition horses. Apart from her seventy-five acres at home, which includes stabling for twenty horses, there is also the use of a further thirteen boxes and an indoor school a couple of miles away. It is here that the breaking and initial education of youngsters is carried out.

The actual fitness preparation of driving horses is in theory less complicated than for other equestrian disciplines. Having said that though you cannot be casual about it because there are several variations within the sport from scurry to marathon, concours d'elegance to

The familiar figure of Cynthia Haydon driving a single hackney.
(Bob Langrish)

Hackneys and, of course, the many breed classes. It follows then that the type of horse will vary enormously from one class to another. The right temperament is always important and for this reason a sound educational foundation from an early age is an investment for future training. The more familiar a horse is with his job before he competes, the less stressful will be the actual competition. A placid nature and a degree of physical and mental stamina will help him endure the rigours of a competitive life. His character will be a first consideration particularly if he is to work alongside other horses in harness – there will always be some animals who work together better than others. Bone and substance are essential for any driving horse because of the load they have to pull. Emphasis should be given to building up the shoulder muscles as they do the most work by pushing against the collar. In Cynthia's case she is fortunate in having her horses very young so that the foundation training can be spread out over two or three years thus reducing the risk of ever doing too much too soon.

In October or November the yearlings have their first introduction to tack and are taught the rudiments of long-reining. Once they become sensible and used to voice commands they are turned away until they are two years old. At this stage, having consolidated on the previous training, they are lunged until they are going confidently and obediently, which may take three to four weeks, before being left again until the following March. As three-year-olds any previous training is repeated and their education is continued to bring them on virtually into showing order. The four-year-olds are brought into work at the same time as the older horses, usually about the end of February or beginning of March.

At the start of a training programme for the four-year-olds and over, the pupils are long-reined for up to threequarters of an hour a day depending on the individual. Lungeing is gradually brought into the daily routine starting with a few minutes a day, building up to about thirty minutes for the 'single' horse and forty-five minutes for the marathon team horse. The difference here is that the 'single' horse is aimed at an exhibition class while the marathon team horses are expected to pull a load of about a ton for eight to twelve miles on the open road. Although the lungeing work never includes cantering they are made to use themselves properly at the trot. The use of an indoor school helps to teach the horses to become obedient to the voice before they are taken on the roads.

It is not practice in this yard to ride any of the horses but as Cynthia explains, it is a matter of personal preference and indeed many people do ride and drive the same horse. Whilst it does offer a change in the horses' routine there may well be instances when it proves to be counter-productive to their education. During the time these horses are in work they are never turned out because, in Cynthia's words, 'it takes the bloom off them'.

The show season for these horses begins in May, usually with the Royal Windsor Show. When Cynthia was showing a full season they would have around thirty shows a year, the climax being the Horse of the Year Show at Wembley. More recently, though, the Haydons have curtailed their competing activities and select just a few shows to attend when they are not busy teaching or producing the young stock. If there is no competition at the weekend all the horses are rested. However, those horses who have worked on the Saturday would be led out on the Sunday for the benefit of their circulation.

Most shows involve two or three days so the practice is to travel to the competition two days before the class begins in order to get the horses settled in and to allow time for preparing the vast amount of equipment. The actual routine at a competition is kept as near as possible to that employed at home with due regard to the feeding times being scheduled around class times. The horses' water supply is never restricted at any time.

Feeding habits are kept as traditional as possible using crushed oats, chaff, bran, sugar-beet and linseed as the regular diet. Racehorse nuts are fed to many of the working horses and apart from cod liver oil which the foals get and salt for the horses in work, no other additives are considered necessary. If, however, it is felt that a competition horse needs it, glucose is added to one feed a day.

Emphasis is placed on the shoeing of each horse, the weight of shoe being dependent on the work that he has to do. Whereas some people believe in the old-fashioned idea that 'weight makes action', Cynthia explains that this is purely a fallacy which in practice creates a heavy, cloddy action. In making the horse pick its feet up he consequently loses elegance, the opposite effect to what you should aim for. A light shoe of between eleven and fourteen ounces is most common, although some horses may need as much as eighteen ounces on each foot. Those who believe in using a heavy shoe to create a high action may use as much as two pounds on each foot.

A blacksmith who lives in Sussex usually makes concave or flat iron shoes for the Haydons then travels to their home in Gloucestershire to shoe the horses. Where a horse has a high action, as in the case of a Hackney, it is recommended that the weight in the shoe be kept in the toe and tapered away from the heel to produce or encourage progressive action. In the summer, plastic pads are fitted to the front feet of the marathon horses and plain Mordax studs are used on the outside of each shoe to help the horses grip during competitions.

The general maintenance duties which surround a yard of competition driving horses are probably twice as many as for riding horses. The upkeep of the carriages alone requires skilled labour such as wheelwrights, and there is also the care of the harness to attend to.

There are no doubt many competent riders who have never had any experience of harnessing and coupling a horse, but who might like to try. If you do aspire to this fascinating sport then it would be wise, to say the least, to seek professional guidance right at the start. Not only will you be taught the rudiments of driving but also, and equally important, the principles of preparing the right animal for the chosen class. In this way both you and your horse will get as much out of the sport as possible.

13 Long-Distance Riding

Pam James

This sport has been enjoying increasing popularity with riders of all ages in recent years, and it comes as no surprise to find that we, as a nation, field internationally successful teams to compete both at home and overseas. One of these more experienced competitors is Pam James who, having been riding all her life, has only latterly confined herself to the preparation of the horse for participation in long-distance rides.

Unlike the other experts in previous chapters, Pam is an owner/groom with the minimum of facilities for her horses and a modestly low budget on which to operate. This chapter then contrasts with others in its example of management and preparation for competition and offers proof that despite strict financial constraints it is quite possible, with dedication and determination, to compete successfully on equal terms with other riders. That is, of course, providing the preparation is as thorough and as well planned.

Pam's first opportunity to ride in an event came about from a chance meeting with Saxon, a Thoroughbred Welsh Cob with a tough constitution that enabled him to live out whilst in work without losing any condition. This had to be Pam's first consideration when she went to buy him because at that time the only facility she had was a field without any shelter whatsoever. It wasn't long before she discovered that Saxon was not a keen jumper, so long-distance riding provided a welcome alternative to their competitive pursuits. Pam subsequently studied the sport thoroughly until she felt she knew enough to make an attempt at preparing Saxon for his first ride. From that day Pam has been spurred on by the challenge which this sport presents. Since 1975 she has ridden in seven Golden Horseshoe Rides across Exmoor and represented Great Britain in international rides abroad.

The ideal type of long-distance horse is Arab or part bred, but preferably not a Thoroughbred. He should be of a calm nature and not waste precious energy by burning it up with excitement or misbehaviour. He will need a tough constitution to endure a lengthy journey over different types of countryside sometimes in foul weather conditions and perhaps on his own. He should be no higher than 16 h.h., but anything from a Welsh mountain pony to a 15.3 h.h. horse of virtually any mixture of breeding will, if he has the right temperament for the job, usually prove as good as the next horse.

Some long-distance riders would recommend three to four years to train a novice horse up to the standard required for 100-mile rides. Pleasure rides over a distance of 15−20 miles are the starting point for long-distance riders after which you might attempt a 20−25 mile qualifier at 6.5−7 mph. The next level would be a 25−50 mile ride taken at 7−8 mph. Once you have successfully completed these you should be ready to undertake a 50−100 miler which is actually a race.

The Golden Horseshoe Ride is to long-distance riders what Wembley is to the show rider and what Badminton is to the event rider. To enter for this ultimate challenge, which is held at the end of the spring season, one has to

The loneliness of the long-distance rider.

have qualified in one of the numerous qualifying events held around the country throughout the year. These are run under the rules of the governing body of the sport – the Long-Distance Riding Group of the British Horse Society. All affiliated long-distance rides are carefully monitored by officials who, together with veterinary surgeons, scrutinise and record the condition of every horse so fitness preparation cannot be too thorough. Horses are eliminated if they show any indication that they are not fit enough to continue on a ride once the vet has examined them at one of the vetting sessions which take place before, during and after the ride. The quality of fitness is quickly detected by checking the heart rate, respiration and by testing the horse for dehydration.

Pam is fortunate in many ways to have the hills surrounding the Forest of Dean on which to prepare her horses. They provide ideal tests of the horses' stamina whilst developing their surefootedness over terrain which in places can be rough. It teaches them to cope with the natural hazards of the countryside that they will have to face during competitions over unfamiliar territory.

The first qualifying rounds for the Golden Horseshoe Ride take place in the middle of March so the horses' preparation for these events begins in early January. When the horses first come in they are wormed, their teeth are rasped and any clipping or trimming is done. The first three weeks of training is spent walking, beginning with half an hour on day one and gradually increasing to one and a half hours a day by the beginning of the fourth week. Unlike other disciplines, these horses are not ridden 'on the bit' as such but encouraged to balance themselves by finding their own footing and establishing their individual rhythm and cadence. As the horse's fitness develops so too will the harmony between horse and rider, building an understanding on which optimum performance is founded without placing undue stress on the horse. It should be borne in mind throughout training that the competition itself sets a certain speed at which you should compete. You will incur penalties if you have not measured your horse's mph correctly. Every horse has a pace or paces at which he prefers to travel and it is up to the rider to make the best of them to achieve the required results.

At the start of the second month of training, the horses begin trotting, firstly on fairly level land, until they are able to trot up hills. This must be done gradually and the rider should play it by ear as to the distance over which the horse can travel at any one time without straining himself unduly. The horse should always be watched as to sweating, bearing in mind the type of clip. Some sweating on the neck is desirable but if the horse is pushed too much too soon this extra exertion will probably show by the horse sweating under and behind the saddle. What is not required is a fatigued horse returning home sweating profusely. This is particularly undesirable at this stage of training because condition lost now will be twice as difficult to replace when the faster work is introduced.

By the end of February or the beginning of March, the horse should be fit enough to do some cantering within the hour and a half daily exercise. The competition itself calls for some long canters, which is another reason for you to memorize the ideal tempo of each horse's paces. Obviously the amount of cantering a horse needs will depend on the individual but generally speaking Pam aims at cantering for five minutes, walking for three minutes and repeating this process twice more during one day's work. Her objective is to build up the canter periods to twelve minutes in the final training session before the big ride. She does, however, only adopt this system in the final month of training before the main ride. Although several long-distance riders use interval training once their horses have begun their canter work, as a system of training it is open to variations. Basically, though, if you do follow the principles of interval training you should be taking pulse and respiration rates both during and after work. The optimum rates should be: pulse – 64 beats per minute, and respiration – 32 breaths per minute. It is important to have an intimate knowledge of each horse's rates because they are checked by vets throughout the competition. Pam usually takes them after each canter and again twenty minutes later. By monitoring the recovery rates she can build up the canter work according to the horse's progress and at the last canter session before the main competition, i.e. The Golden Horseshoe Ride, the canter periods should each be over twelve minutes.

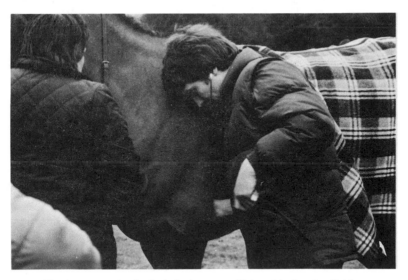

The heart rate is checked during a qualifying ride for the Golden Horseshoe.

During March and April, Pam competes in local riding club events and hunter trials to add variety to the fitness programme. She does not jump the horse too near to a ride for fear of injury although she admits she would love to do more. Whilst her training methods offer a programme of 'peaks and troughs' rather than one long exercise, she aims to be able to complete a three and a half hour ride the week before a major ride. In the final week, with the possible exception of a short canter about the middle of the week to act as a 'pipe-opener', Pam reduces the work just enough to keep the horse ticking over. If during the second half of the training programme a horse becomes tense, Pam will give him a couple of days off and turn him out instead of riding. Often by travelling the horse to a different location for his training he will be given the change he needs to prevent staleness. Alternatively, lungeing is a useful form of exercise apart from its aid to schooling. Unfortunately Pam does not have enough flat land on which to lunge or school her horses but she suggests that anyone who does can use it for performing simple schooling movements such as circles, serpentines, rein-back and change of lead for cantering. She recommends these exercises because they are extremely helpful for suppling the horse and engaging his hocks, but, of course, they must be carried out correctly: a horse should not, for example, be asked to work in very small circles which can damage joints. Proper schooling, she stresses, will also improve the horse's balance by taking the weight off his forehand. This in turn will reduce the concussion to his forelegs, help him to cope with uneven terrain and hopefully teach him to look after himself. If you are constantly holding on to him he will invariably shorten his stride and stiffen over a long distance: the opposite to what you should be aiming to achieve.

Usually towards the end of March and during April there are both 20−25-mile pleasure rides and 40-mile qualifying rides, while in September 30-mile rides offer a build-up to the major event. Pam finds they are a very important part of the fitness programme. Not only do they offer a guide to your horse's fitness but also they ensure that you are achieving the required speed which is easily mis-timed especially if you do your training alone.

The routine at home revolves around the horses' work and Pam's busy schedule as a mother and owner/groom. Whilst the horses are in work they are given one rest day per week. If a horse takes part in a competition then his rest day will coincide with the day following the event. Feed times on a normal day are at 7.30 a.m., 12.30 p.m., 6.00 p.m., and, if necessary, a fourth feed is given at 11 p.m. Apart from conventional feedstuffs such as oats, bran and sugar-beet, Pam feeds nuts and Bailey's mixed feed as well as additives such as liquid molasses, seaweed, calcium/salt mixture and Epsom salts. Once fast work has started an average diet would comprise 8lbs oats, 6lbs Bailey's, 1lb bran, 3lbs sugar-beet, 3lbs nuts plus an ounce of salt/calcium mixture and 2oz of seaweed per day.

At competitions the competitor's schedule is pro- grammed by the organisers. The horse's management on the day is in some ways different to that of other endur- ance-type horses such as eventers. One of the main differences is in watering the horses because long- distance riding horses are tested for dehydration even before the competition begins. This is known as the 'pinch test' whereby a fold of skin in the middle of the neck is pinched briefly. If the skin, once released, takes longer than four seconds to relax the competitor is penalised. Should that interval extend to ten seconds the horse will be eliminated. Clearly then, with such a strict examination it is up to you to ensure that the horse is offered a drink at regular intervals. If you travel alone it will mean stopping during the journey. During the competition the horse is offered about a gallon of water at regular intervals. Pam finds that on the whole her horse will not drink before he has completed about twenty miles. Throughout the ride he may drink as much as four to five gallons. This is in strict contrast to event horses who traditionally are not allowed a drink for the last hour before they run cross-country until after they have finished and recovered from the exertion. Although long-distance horses do not have to gallop they are working for long periods at a time. It has been found that their body heat quickly raises the water temperature and they do not usually suffer ill-effects such as colic from drinking during exercise. Once the horse has recovered from the ride he is offered half a bucketful of water from time to time until he is drinking in moderation when he can then have water *ad lib.*

Electrolytes are added to the water at this stage but if they put the horse off drinking, plain water is made available.

If the competition is far from home as in the case of the Golden Horseshoe on Exmoor, Pam will travel down the day before to give the horse a chance to settle. A feed is given three to four hours before the ride and hay is available in moderation up to the time of tacking up. Immediately after the ride and once the horse has been made comfortable he is offered a bran mash. If all is well he is then given a feed made up of half his normal ration. Finally, at about 10.30 p.m., providing his appetite is normal and he shows no signs of distress, he is fed a full ration of concentrates. The day after a competition Pam either rides the horse for an hour at the walk or leads him out.

Once a week Pam's horses are given a rest day when they are turned out for a few hours, weather permitting. Every day they get an hour or so in the paddock, before or after their work because Pam rides either in the morning or the afternoon depending on her commitments.

Roughing off at the end of the season, which is usually after a major ride such as the Golden Horseshoe, will normally take about a week. The summer holiday usually lasts from mid-May to the second week of July. Preparation then begins all over again for the autumn season which climaxes with the Goodwood or Black Mountain Ride.

Whilst the horses' shoes are a normal road shoe, Pam does recommend the use of pads because they save the sole from bruising when the horse is going across rough country. Remember: lamenesses and wounds incur penalties which can lead to elimination, so any precaution is worthwhile. Backs, too, should be protected from long periods of weight-carrying. Pam applies methylated spirits twice a week but warns that if used too much or on sensitive skin it can cause the skin to become dry and flaky.

Obviously, in order that a rider can actually ride the horse for such long distances he must be fairly fit himself. Whilst riding each day will develop a certain amount of fitness, the rider should ensure that he will not be unduly fatigued from riding long distances. Pam swims twice a week to improve her stamina and respiration because she doesn't feel that riding alone will prepare her adequately for hours in the saddle. Apart from the obvious patience required of a long-distance rider in preparing the horse over weeks and many miles, he must have a sensitive feel for the horse's ability and never be tempted into pushing him beyond his limits. Experience and common sense should tell the rider when to stop before the horse becomes distressed.

Long-distance riding is the one sport which riders of all ages can enjoy and one which is comparatively inexpensive. Providing your horse's preparation is carefully planned to meet the fitness standards required and you yourself can do the horse justice, you should have years of competitive fun out of what is a rapidly expanding equestrian sport in this country.

14 Conclusion

We are all aware of the tremendous pleasure to be gained from horses and it is hoped that this book has gone some way towards encouraging riders to improve their standard of equestrianism by striving for better performances with their horses. Whilst horses enable us to participate in sports their generosity should never be abused by mis-handling. We are, after all, taking a wild animal and training it for our own pleasure which is something we should not forget. Higher standards of horsemanship are gained by practice together with a willingness to learn and adapt to changes and new experiences. We know that every horse will offer a new situation in some way during his fitness programme, be it with work, feeding or during the competition itself. A trained eye will recognise the need for change in any situation but I sincerely hope that the previous chapters have brought to your attention the many aspects involved in the preparation of horses for competition. What we are all aiming for in every discipline is a fit horse who is comfortably capable of achieving a specific performance for which he has been trained. The leading question is: how do we know when a horse is fit? We know that each discipline requires a different type and level of fitness. It is then up to us to adapt these requirements into a training schedule for each horse taking into account the many factors which comprise an individual programme, beginning of course with the type of animal we have. Each horse has his own capabilities and limitations, so first of all we must be sure we understand his potential and be able to channel his own natural talent towards his ultimate performance.

Competitions are the obvious testing ground for a horse's fitness but, as has been pointed out, 'dry runs' prior to the main event will help us to ensure that we are on target and if necessary we can make any changes in good time to encourage improved performance. What we are looking for in every case is to complete a particular competitive exercise comfortably within the horse's scope and without causing him undue stress, so that he can recover from an exertion in a safe period of time and not lose more condition than that which cannot easily be replaced. A fatigued horse is one who has not been adequately prepared for a specific task and is therefore not fit to compete. Hopefully he will not suffer too much and the rider will learn from the mistake, taking care to alter the horse's preparation accordingly even if it means returning to slower work for a while and perhaps missing a competition or two.

The featured experts have offered some background to their successes, which, as can be seen, are based upon months of dedicated preparation and attention to every detail involved in fittening horses. Any rider who has enjoyed the pleasures of a competitive achievement will have experienced the satisfaction of completing an event on a well-trained horse. Whether that horse's fitness was all it could be or how nearly his potential was realised in each competition is something for the rider to evaluate. Each training session should have a goal to work towards followed by an appraisal with a trainer whenever possible. Competitions offer the rider and horse the opportunity to measure every factor which contributes to the results of each performance. The old adage 'One's own geese are always swans', runs so very true with horses, for we can never tell how good ours are until they are tried against others. All the best training and preparation in the world cannot be fully appreciated until it has been proved in competition.

No matter who we are, we all need someone to help with training of both horse and rider. Regular coaching is probably more important from the horse's point of view in disciplines which involve dressage and jumping, although of course we can all accommodate improvements in our riding. Whilst those of us with limited funds may not be able to afford tuition from a top trainer it is worth saving to find someone whom we respect and with whom we get along to help us from time to time. Even once a month is better than nothing if the rider is to improve and indeed lose bad habits which so easily set in if they are not pointed out.

Whatever your choice of horse sport and whichever system of training you adopt always put your horse first and remember to thank him for the enjoyment he gives you. No matter what the result of the competition itself you will have derived much satisfaction from taking part. The fact that you have planned a programme and reached the competition on a sound horse, fit and eager to compete will have its own rewards. The joy of success is just the icing on the cake to be enjoyed for as long as it lasts. The effort of reaching the top is one thing but staying there is much harder. No matter what your level of ambition it is always thrilling to bring home a rosette and a happy, healthy horse.

May I then conclude by wishing all competitors the very best of luck in your chosen sport and hoping that through careful preparation your horses will always be fit to compete.

APPENDIX — Useful Addresses

Listed below are the addresses of the governing bodies for the seven equestrian disciplines covered in this book.

Dressage

Dressage Group
British Horse Society
British Equestrian Centre
Stoneleigh
Kenilworth
Warwickshire
CV8 2LR
Tel: 0203-55241

Show-Jumping

British Show-Jumping Association
British Equestrian Centre
Kenilworth
Warwickshire
CV8 2LR
Tel: 0203-552511

Horse Trials

Horse Trials Group
British Horse Society
British Equestrian Centre
Kenilworth
Warwickshire
CV8 2LR
Tel: 0203-52241

Parent body to the preceding organisations:

British Equestrian Federation
British Equestrian Centre
Stoneleigh
Kenilworth
Warwickshire
CV8 2LR
Tel: 0203-52241

Polo

Hurlingham Polo Association
Ambersham Farm
Midhurst
West Sussex
GU29 0BX
Tel: 07985-277

Showing

The National Light Horse Breeding Society
8 Market Square
Westerham
Kent
TN16 1AW
Tel: 0959-63867

British Show Pony Society
124 Green End Road
Sawtry
Huntingdon
Cambs
TEl: 08322-2041

There are many different breed societies with which one may register a horse for showing and for qualifying purposes.

Driving

British Driving Society
10 Marley Avenue
New Milton
Hants
BH25 5LJ
Tel: 0425-616338

Long-Distance Riding

Long Distance Riding Group
British Horse Society
British Equestrian Centre
Stoneleigh
Kenilworth
Warwickshire
CV8 2LR
Tel: 0203-52241

It is recommended that you apply for details to the relevant secretary before the start of the season and ensure that your membership is valid each year before you enter qualifying classes. Failure to register yourself and your horse before entering a qualifying competition is an offence under the rules of that organisation and can result in disciplinary action being taken.

Index